MW01519466

*...on your
Support*

[signature]

WOMANIZER

The following people/things made this book possible in one way or another
(and listed in no particular order)

God Almighty
My lovely wife (My Muse)
Byron II (Stay focused!)
Brandon (Stand up and be heard!)
Bryce (Lord bless us all!)
Dear Ole Dad (The Worlds greatest teacher)
Mom (you always right)
Pastor Twymon
Mike Veney
My Little brother Myron Williams
My baby brother Kenny Williams
Adam Rogers
Collin Love
E-Bone thanks for believing
Heyward R. Cooke & Moses Overton for listening
Mike Mack my neighbor and computer whiz
Divine Culture for the science of life
Art Forest for the wisdom
Stephanie Hammonds, ESQ and her mentoring
All the Gregory Women
Jerry Doby Public Relations
Lastly, to all the women I did wrong, Karma paid me back big-time!

To my god-mother(s)
Octavia Wicks and Caroline Mc Cants
May they rest in peace

WOMANIZER

Thee Uncomfortable Truth about Men and Marriage

Only Real men through the Word can train other men to become real men.
"As iron sharpens iron, so one man sharpens another." Proverbs 27:17 (NIV)

By The Bestselling Author
BYRON "BIG-NAZ" WILLIAMS

Published By
Manage Me Productions, LLC

Publication Data

Williams, Byron 1970-

WOMANIZER
By Byron "Big-Naz" Williams
Poems by Rhythm of Life (Kenneth J. Williams)
Cover Design Mc Tech Computers

Paperback Advice

ISBN: Softcover   978-1-9703881-5-5

  1.   Self Help—Dating and Marriage
  2.   Non-fiction
  3.   Humor

Manage Me Productions, LLC
Fax: 248.545.6180
Email: *Bignaz228@aol.com*
http://byronwilliams.org

This book was printed in the United States of America.

To order additional copies of this book, contact:
Xlibris Corporation
1-888-795-4274
www.Xlibris.com
Orders@Xlibris.com
29746

Contents

ABOUT THE AUTHOR

I'VE BEEN THERE and done that! Over the last decade I've managed to complete my Bachelors in Mass Communications, get married, play a short stint of pro basketball, develop a publishing firm, wrote my first Best Seller at 30 yrs old, Provided Personal Protection to Megastar Eminem for 9mos., raise 3 sons, coach little league Football and Baseball, publish my second book at 35yrs. old, and nourish a ten year marriage. How? I credit God and my supportive wife. I would have nothing without them. The purpose of writing this book is to enlighten men on solutions and or strategies in preparation for marriage. I have no intention of appearing as a relationship expert but an opinionated, imperfect husband. Fortunately, I share the same insight of other husbands around the world when it comes to dealing with life. In today's society, husbands have taken a docile role in their home in order to not interrupt a peaceful environment. Therefore, a man with a closed mouth refuses to be heard. He has become a human bobble head. However these husbands will complain during their weekly "woman hater" meetings, and then return home with no resolution. I have elected myself as the mouthpiece for husbands and bachelors everywhere. Many might not agree with the male point of view, but generally the examples I present; they're all true!

I've always considered myself a writer and excelled in creative expression. My books are often criticized for blending real life and Christianity. My works represent real situations. **Those who are easily offended should put the book down or give it back to whom you borrowed it from. Life is brutally honest and so am I.**

I grew up in the heart of Detroit, raised by both parents. My peers often teased us as the neighborhood rich kids. That stigma is still with my brothers and me until this day. I guess it safe to say that I've been womanizing since the age 14 yrs. old. I learned early in life, that women like nice things. I can recall a time when my family ran a neighborhood flea market on the weekends and I was responsible for the set up. We sold mostly female items from perfume to jewelry. The neighborhood girls would frequent the flea market just to browse. I would watch them closely to see what they admire the most and later surprised them with a gift. I would only supply gifts to those girls whom I thought were cute. Unfortunately, the word spread to other females who never gave me the time of day. The two girls, whom I gave jewelry, discovered they had the same identical rings. They confronted me and asked whom I liked the most, and I said "both". They were mad for a short time but they forgave me when I gave them more costume jewelry. This caused me to get more intimate with my female peers. I learned that jewels can lead to dry humping. These young girls assumed that I was buying the jewels and perfume from my family flea market. The thought of me spending money on them, made them feel special. Needless to say my Momma caught wind of what was going on and shut me down quick. Momma counted the inventory and noticed things were missing and called me on the situation. I lied of course, but momma knew. As the summer went by, I grew tired of the young girl games and took notice of my best friend's older cousin. We'll call this older woman "Tammy". Tammy was 18yrs old, and hot to trot. I was always mature for my age in stature and personality. Tammy took a liking to me and called me her little boyfriend. My best friend at that time was going up north to visit his cousin Tammy and invited me to go. I went, and we ended up staying the night there with her family. The adults went out that night and hung late. All that day Tammy and I were eyeing each other. Finally, that evening we were all watching a movie under the covers and Tammy began to fondle my manhood which led to big things. Tammy leaned over and whispered these exact words, "Come on". She grabbed me by the hand and led me to her bedroom. She then pulled up her night gown with no underwear and beckoned me to come over. I then proceeded to take off my pants. I then reached into my wallet for the long awaited use of this condom I bought weeks before. As I rolled on the condom, Tammy turns on the radio. Just as I inserted my manhood, the song "Let's Hear it for the Boy!" by Deneice Williams is playing. I was officially a man now as I rowed and stroked up her raging river only to be tossed from the boat before the song ended. Luckily I was wearing a life Jacket. I was hooked from that point on sexually. I was 14yrs. old and she was 18yrs old. That was the only time we had sex. After being brought on board by an older woman, teen girls could never work. They played games, and older women knew what they wanted.

Years later when I went off to college, the women became easier to conquer. If you were an athlete, sex was automatic. I was the #1 basketball recruit at Olivet College my freshman year. I really expanded my sexual escapades to the extremes. It became a matter of when I wanted to have sex, and not with whom. College women were free for the first time to explore their womanhood and I was there to welcome them with an open zipper. I satisfied women of all nations ranging from the American Barbie Doll, Asians, Italians, Dutch and bunch of African American Women. It's not so that I needed the sex, it was just available at my demand. These women aimed to please me. They bought me things, paid my bills, cooked for me, and took me shopping. All they wanted me to do is bring them to several orgasmic pleasures. That's something I loved to do. **I was known for over satisfying a woman. I always believe that a man should give a woman an abundance of orgasms in a short amount of time.** The more orgasms she has, the less competition you'll have. I prided myself in teaching women not to be selfish sexually. I taught them to reciprocate fulfillment.

It's funny how the table turns. At the age of 19yrs. old, I felt sexually invincible. I was bringing women to tearful orgasms, sexual dehydration and mental breakdowns. That was my style. I felt it was time to elevate my game to another level. At that stage in my life no one woman could handle me mentally or sexually. I would often read many relationship and sexual books on satisfying women. I had the charm, knowledge and well endowment every woman desired. I finally met my match, her name was Nancy. Nancy was 38yrs old, a single kinky corporate executive. I met Nancy on the freeway. I was home for the summer from college, when I saw her on the freeway. I was driving on I-96, when I noticed this gorgeous red-bone African American woman on the side of me. I blew my horn at her to get her attention; she gazed at me with a smile. I rolled down my window to ask her name. Sounds corny at 70 mph? It gets better! I asked her to pullover so we can talk. She said, "I don't know you, you might be crazy!" I used the college charm and said "I'm home from college, and I want to get to know you!" She said, "Okay, make it quick!" We parked on the side of the road, with me at the rear. As I got out of my awesome Mustang, I could see her peering at me while biting her bottom lip, with a look of lust in her eyes. I approached the car wearing dark shades, and my shirt unbuttoned showing off my then six pack and bulging chest. She said, "Let me see your eyes." I took off the shades. And she replied "Ooh Sexy, but so young". I asked her name as she says, "Nancy". I tell her my name as trucks are blowing damn near running me over. I didn't care I wanted to conquer this woman. I got the courage to request her phone number and she declined. I said, "I'm risking my life on the side of the road and can't get your number?' She chuckled and said, "Give me yours." I said, "I'm home visiting my momma for the summer. Please don't call after midnight." She chuckled again and said okay. We politely shook hands. I turned and walked back to my car. I was excited. I landed a mature honey. Once I arrived at momma house, momma was watering her outdoor plants. Immediately momma says, "Some woman named Nancy called you! She sounds like and older woman! I don't like all these women calling my house." I excitedly responded, "Momma did you get her number!" She replies, "Boy I ain't your secretary!" There was a moment of silence and then momma said "The number is on the table." I gave her a kiss and a hug and said thanks momma. Immediately I called Nancy to set up date for that evening. Before I left, my momma asked me, "What are you going to do about your girlfriend when she calls?" I said "Momma, cover for me. Tell her I'm out playing ball!" Momma said she wasn't getting involved in that mess. As I got in the car, momma shook her head shamelessly with a grin on her face as to say my boy is grown. I proceeded to Nancy's house verifying directions, calling from a huge bag cell phone. When I arrived, Nancy had already planned the whole evening. I'll never forget this as long as I live. Right before we exited the car to see the movie, Nancy questioned me this, "What do you want from me Byron?" I said, "I want to learn from you mentally as well as physically." She said okay. We got the tickets watched the show as she did subtle rubs on my inner thighs. When the movie ended, we went back to her place. She put on some Jazz music as she began to whip up some stir fried chicken. As I patiently waited, she came out with two shot glasses and a bottle of cognac. She made a toast, "To learning new things." She took the Hennessy straight to the head, and I sipped one taste, she said "swallow it whole". She then went back to the kitchen and left me with my chest on fire. That was the first time I had ever tasted Hennessey. After dinner, we retreated to her Bedroom to watch movies. As we lay on her leopard skin bed she began to get very aroused. She led the mood. She grabbed my hand and placed it between her thighs where the wetness had soaked through her blue jeans. I was totally amazed at her excessive lubrication. After much foreplay, she excused herself to the rest room where she changed into a negligee. She soon appeared in this tiny leopard gown barely covering her rear. She began to purr like a cat in a slow stroll to the King size bed where I lay. She crawled into the bed just like a large lioness. She unbuttoned my pants slowly but with force. She slowly reached for my underwear, and I rushed to take them off. She then took off my shirt and began to eat on me like I was dessert. She licked me clean. I then returned the favor, and then she rolled me over and showed me her best impression of a cowgirl on a bucking stallion. Ironically, I was holding on for dear life. **This was a woman out to overly please me in a short amount of time.** The positions were endless; I could barely keep up with this old girl. Later that night she kicked me out only to never return my phone calls. I thought I was in love. She was the best I ever had encountered in my young sexual prime. I thought about her night and day. I couldn't function. I turned away women advances because Nancy had me wide open. I would call her several times a day. I would look for her in the day time with a flash light! I finally reached a mental breakdown about her and noticed that she taught me mentally as well as physically. She gave me what I asked for in that one stand. She also did to me what I had been doing to women all along, "Love them and Leave them!" I had women mentally and physically strung out over me and Nancy gave me a taste of my own medicine. She never really got to know me as a person. In retrospect I never took the time know my victims either. Nancy taught me that sex is easy but communication is necessary. There will come a time and place when all womanizer will get neutralized. Nancy was just my first lesson. Enjoy the book.

CHAPTER 1

From boys to men

AS THE WHEELS TURN FROM BIG WHEELS TO
AUTOMOBILES
BOYS TRANSFORM INTO MEN
TONKA TRUCKS FALL OUT OF OUR HANDS
BECAUSE OUR DESIRES ARE BIGGER
OUR DAY DREAMS TURN INTO WET DREAMS
AS OUR SAND BOX BUDDIES START TO LOOK LIKE TEEN
SUPERMODELS
OUR TASTE FOR SIPPY CUPS TURNS INTO THRIST FOR
YOUNG LUV
PLAYFUL WORDS AND PUNCHING TURNS INTO
MYSTERIOUS TOUCHING
AND LATE NIGHT CONVERSATIONS
AS BOYS TRANSFORM TO MEN OUR LIKES TURN INTO
LOVE.

By Rhythm of Life

E VEN BEFORE BIRTH, an infant male is expected to grow up and conquer the world. He is taught that he should be tough, and never cry. This especially applies in front of women, because it shows a sign of weakness. Some women on the other hand know this and tend to capitalize on a man emotions every chance she gets. And women wonder why men don't communicate well. Men are protecting their feelings and usually don't like their mate too see them emotionally disturbed. However, most men are able to confide in the first woman they ever met, "MOM". Why? She'll listen, nurture him and give him confidence. Ladies take heed to this valuable point in making preparations to satisfying your man. Gentlemen don't expect your mate to act like your mother in every instance, besides that some sick fantasy anyway. It's rare that a female will match the standards of mom. Ladies, if he wants you to meet his mom it could be serious.

Men are simple creatures that women and society force to be difficult. Prime example, as the old nursery rhyme says, "Girls are made of sugar and spice and everything nice." "Boys are made Frogs and Snails, and Puppy dog tails." Men are tired of being called anything slimy, and labeled attachments to a butt. Do you hear me Ladies?

As a boy grows older he'll find how difficult a woman can truly be in a relationship. The first crisis boys usually incur is around 6 yrs.-8 yrs. old on Valentines Day. A young boy can be scarred for a long time if the girl is too harsh. Many men have stated that girls have hurt their feelings on Valentines Day in school when passing out cards. Being called ugly, fat, dirty, and my personal favorite, too dark, scarred them. Damn pretty boys! And sometimes these girls weren't the prettiest, but these boys thought they were special. The boys accepted them for who they were. But Nooo! Not the girls!

These same girls grew up being taught by their moms and Old Maid Aunts to make sure that a man always treats you well, provide and oh yeah pay all the bills. At an early age, women are taught to be takers and that men should provide no matter what. "If that man can't provide, then he's not a man!" What the hell's is that all about? He's probably recovering from the last taker he encountered. We live in an era when women are so independent, that it turns most gentlemen callers away. Some women are stuck on what she has done for herself without a man. She actually convinces her ego that a man is useless. I believe that most women of this characteristic were hurt during a past relationship which induced an over zealous attitude about being successful. Once she reached this plateau by using her wits, and a dildo to get her through the nights, she decided she would make men pay for her loneliness. In her own mind she has created the perfect ménage trios featuring herself, her money and her dildo. Although no man is present, her sex toy represents the male counterpart with no emotional baggage. Many women live in denial of being so-called "Strong Independent" women. Most become wealthy but bitter, old maids, or recruited as lesbians. The way to solve those problems is to stop canceling mans love out of the equation.

Men have learned that some women truly believe in the" Knight in Shinning Armor", and want to be swept off their feet. Keep dreaming ladies, because your

Knight could be in a rusted Pinto. Understand that situations do change for the better. If most women can look past the rusted Pinto and acknowledge the gentleman, it's possible he can become anything he wants and everything she dreamed. The sooner a woman realizes that a man who receives support and encouragement can accomplish anything, the better. In turn, she usually can get whatever she desires. That's a hint. It's that simple. However, if your man is a bum and not working toward a goal, this doesn't apply.

CHAPTER 2

Living Single

I'M LIVING SINGLE FOR ALL THE WRONG REASONS
THE SEX, FREEDOM, NO COMMITMENT
NO RULES, NO FUSSING, NO PROBLEMS
BUT IT COMES WITH A PENALTY
AND THE PENALTY IS LONELINESS

By Rhythm of Life

T HE BEST TIMES of a man's life occurs as a bachelor. It means freedom to roam the earth. Freedom to do whatever and whomever he likes. Nothing on earth can fill the void of Being a strong, physically fit, financially secure, who is a sexy straight bachelor that can knock the lid off a woman's orgasmic chamber every time. We will call him **Dick Dynamite**. Ladies we're talking USDA prime cut beef. And Ladies stop fronting! You seek Dick at work, at church, at nightclubs, and most of all in your dreams. Sadly, Dick's been right there in front of your face the whole time. Unfortunately, he may not have the job title she can be proud of, but at least he's a working Dick. Most women miss the opportunity of landing a decent man if his title is sub par. A woman allows her friends to pick her men by peer pressure. Dick could be an aspiring writer by night and a garbage man by day. His wages may be meager but his efforts are momentous toward succeeding beyond hauling garbage. Unfortunately, he'll be turned away from time to time because of his job title. But when his dream career takes off, she'll be the first of many in line to say I always believed in you! A woman's impatience helps mold this mans attitude into a "Hit and Run" or "Wham Bam thank you mam! Dick has no time for women insecurities, and or being shamed by his way of survival. Although he works hard, she may feel he doesn't bring enough to the table. Sometimes Dick can be very much needed in the bedroom but unappreciated at a business luncheon. Most women want their Dick seen and not heard.

When a man is single, he has power. He has few worries and minor responsibilities. He's in his prime of life for history making moments that he can recall in later days. He's ALIVE! Dick Dynamite has the ability to spend money in excess without a conscience in a single bound. He can leave females suspended in mid air with his savvy and sexual fulfillment. Dick Dynamite has a mouthpiece of a lesbian turned thespian whom is a world champion of spelling bees. Women Please! Skilled in conversation and keeps a woman in anticipation of his knowledgeable words. He can take a tool of articulation and cause any women heart palpitation through clitoral stimulation and have her mind, body and spirit exasperated. Wow! Dick Dynamite women hate to love him, and love to hate him.

Surprisingly, he can also hold a temporary commitment. That's right, temporary. Meaning 30 days to 7yrs of his precious time designated for one woman, simultaneously. We're talking dating, not marriage. This event is possible but rare. Usually Dick prefers a culmination rolodex of women whom he is at their disposal. Dick Dynamite has exquisite taste in women. Only the finest, can hold his arm. They must be sharp, curvy, witty, exotic, sexual, and have some charm. Why so many women? He's building a complete woman with bits and pieces of each. Promiscus? He's just a safe sexual being. Why? He doesn't want any mishaps that would hinder his program. AIDS, STD's, and Kids are not part of his plan. Deep within, Dick Dynamite is seeking this perfect woman to find out she doesn't exist. Therefore he builds Brides of Frankenstein. In order for this operation to be successful he'll need to befriend a variety of women, thus creating a harem. It's not done intentionally. Its just ingredients to Dick Dynamite's recipe to get what he wants. Dick acquires these "wants" through giving, taking, teaching, pleasing and lastly learning. Women are the greatest teachers in life and they don't even realize it. For every woman whom has failed with a man, she has better prepped him for the next woman. Men usually look back on those experiences after the fact. Sadly, women get the short end of Dick, unless you're on the receiving end of getting this new and improved Dick. Then it's even.

Cheaters always win: Let's be honest, if someone is dating, there's no such thing as cheating. Remember, Cheating only counts when you're married. Besides, cheating is over-rated. How is a man supposed to know what he wants in life if he sticks to only one brand of female? Yes men are dogs, some aren't house broken and others choose to do their business elsewhere. I hear guys crying all the time about how their girlfriend is cheating on them. It's open game, and women are just as guilty. Men just get caught and women don't. Women are dogs too, they are just trained to use kitty litter boxes and cover all their crap nice and neatly. When women cheat, they tell True Lies. True Lies? Here is a prime example; she leaves the house everyday for work as usual right? At least you think! Baby Girl is on her way to the hotel for a day shrimp, and sex. You sucker! Plus she got paid at work because she used vacation time. Also more women are joining health spas. That's not necessarily good. Single women are using the gym as an excuse to get out the house for sex. That includes married women as well. At first these men support their woman quest for getting that teenage body back. In the beginning, you notice some results in her attendance. She loses a few pounds. When she started out, she weighed 200lbs. It's six months later and she weighs 225 1lbs and got more dimples in her booty than a golf ball. Yes, she is doing leg lifts but it not at the gym. Men need to start snooping around like women do occasionally. Men need to start checking their woman check stubs and get a membership at the gym with her non-exercising ass. Women don't need a reason to violate your privacy; it just comes with the territory. Oh, your woman doesn't do that? When you're sleep; she watching you, going through your wallet, plotting her next move or your next move. You see what Eve did when Adam went to sleep in the Garden of Eden; she took one rib and nagged him to eat the apple by telling him God was wrong. That's another story.

Men if you're insecure, this peace of advice doesn't apply. If you suspect your woman of cheating, don't say anything unless you have absolute proof. You have to build a case with women that will hold up in any Supreme Court or you got nothing. You're only going to make her change her game for the better, by then kick her to the curb. Ladies I know this is hard for you to swallow so gulp twice. Some of you are use to the ingestion. I advise all single men to be upfront with single women by telling them the rules of your game. The rules should be that you are free to see other people. However, men don't be mad when she plays by the rules and does the same. Communication is everything.

Bisexual Women: What the Hell is going on? "She stole my woman!" Women are canceling men out at a tragic rate. Dick Dynamite is an endangered species. The penis is becoming extinct in female life. Men were totally cool with a woman having a vibrator or two. That's as long as the vibrator didn't put him out of business. First rule of thumb, never let her toy be bigger than you. There's nothing worse than a man in the corner crying in the fetal position. If that man isn't working with much, that's a different story. Fellow men, the stock has gone up on "Strap on Dildo's". Some women have totally eliminated meat from their diet in a choice for fish only. Women like what we like more now than ever. It was cool when she liked Football, but now she likes women. Some women have too many secrets. Nobody just turns lesbian or bisexual overnight. It was a thought process somewhere. The sexual lifestyle has evolved from a cave man busting his woman over the head and dragging her back to the cave for some sex; to society posting penises in the missing person slot of the milk carton. It's a shame to hear men admitting they can't find a good woman to marry. I tell men, today's women are like ostriches; they have their head up another good woman's butt. You have to catch them when they come up for air. Even then, you have to talk quick and be meaningful and hopefully she doesn't submerge. The most disturbing part of dating a bisexual woman is that a man and his fantasy, introduced her to it. Now she's stuck. Men don't open Pandora's Box if you're not ready for the literal consequences. Also men, if she gets turned out in your little fantasy, she's gone forever. I've seen guys marry these women and continue the fun only to come home and find his wife calling another woman's name in ecstasy. A woman of that caliber has an insatiable sexual appetite that no one can fulfill. Every man loves a whore, but nobody wants to marry one. However, men do want their wives super freaky exclusively. Men stop being threatened by the dildos, bullets, vibrators, and that new thing with a penis and tongue attached. Women truly are showing men, they don't need us. You better go buy your woman some toys and oils man! Plus be sensual to the touch and caresses. But make sure to satisfy her so well that every time you stroke her, you get a concussion because your butt keeps hitting the back of your head. Or Butch Bertha gone have her and gone. A woman understands a woman. Men have to start reading Redbook, Mademoiselle, and Essence. We still won't understand them, but at least we'll know what they're talking about. Truth of the matter, women see themselves as the treasure. Just beware of the Pu55y Pirates. Pu55y Pirates is that lesbian that pawns a straight man treasures never to be seen again. She cares nothing about your ticket of ownership.

A Mans worth: It has always been about a woman's worth. You heard Alicia Keys. "Let a woman cum first." Yep, then she goes right to sleep. A woman's idea of a man's worth is the amount of his life insurance policy. More men need to step up to their responsibility in life. There are too many punks corrupting women's minds that make it difficult for men whom aren't afraid of commitment. We as men always pursue women. We feel a need to impress women. Our heads are always on the chopping block, ready to roll. Women need to occasionally feel some genuine rejection. **I dare any self proclaimed MAN to step up and make women except you as a treasure.** Men are always cashing in the chips only to lose while she cashes out with another. We have value too! It's the simple things like her paying for dinner sometime. She plans a weekend getaway without hitting you up for a loan the week after. Realistically, you paid for the trip. Ladies I dare you to send your man some flowers to work. On his Birthday, go all out! Get him that stretch limo, expensive dinner and tickets to something he'll enjoy. We do too much for these damn women, not to get any appreciation. Buy him something nice on Father's Day. I know he said, "Don't get me anything!" He is lying! He is mad as hell on the inside when you don't get him something. Why do men say that? Some men don't feel worthy. You let a man not buy his woman a gift or card for her birthday. He'll hear about that for a while. She might even go on strike! He'll have to call in a union rep., because she won't work in the kitchen, the bedroom or the laundry room. The poor man will be walking around for weeks hungry with a hard-on wearing dirty draws. That's a woman's worth! That's just the mere threat of you not respecting her worth. Now that's appreciation. Men don't get worth from women because we don't demand it. We just write it off and complain to our buddies about the lack of appreciation. Women hold the cards, but we can fix the deck. Example: Turn her down for sex sometime, just to shatter her ego. Tell her you have a headache, or you're too tired. It doesn't matter how it's done, just do it. How? Men have to go on strike sometime. Hell, act like you're having a period. Totally ignore her whole being, request, and advances. How? Get some hobbies that don't include her. Another suggestion is empty your gun occasionally when you have a need to shoot off. I'm suggesting masturbation. Don't act like you haven't been there. You probably do it so much you got Copper Tunnel Syndrome.

Please be advised, this is not the hobby I was suggesting. If you eliminate the desire for ejaculation, it will make your strike more reachable. This tactic will only work for so long; so don't fall in love with you. Men have no shame. Women do it all the time. Heed why her sexual strikes last so long. Men are born with an instinctive knowledge of masturbation and appear before they realize it exists. My four year old son has become fascinated with his body to the point where I have to remind him that his wink-wink is not a toy. I recently chastised him of by saying "Stop playing with that thing!" He replied in a firm voice, "When will I get to play with it! When I get married?" I was stunned! Because he was absolutely right! I replied, "If you're lucky, you're wife will play with it for you, or you could end up playing with more than you do now. Let's cross that bridge when you get to it, okay?" He looked at me with somewhat of a confused manly gaze, and said "Okay daddy." The women have toys and we have a joystick stuck on one player. Some women usually call off the strike when the batteries die or the vibrator mysteriously ends up missing. It's too bad men don't have quality toys on the market besides "blow up" dolls. I imagine that would be like making love to your grandma's old couch that is wrapped in plastic. Unfortunately, the one male toy that might be decent is the "Electrical Vagina". It has an extension chord for the electrical outlet. That's got to be like sticking a fork in the socket. The point is, once a man has conquered his sexual urges, he has conquered the relationship. When a woman feels she is not needed physically, she may become insecure. She may think you're cheating, turned gay or don't desire her anymore. If that occurs, you have succeeded in the first steps in gaining a man's worth. Women think we only want them for sex, therefore we must prove them wrong. Eliminate the sex.

We as men need to be complimented by our women from time to time, not nagged. There is a difference. Example of a woman missed compliment: "Baby, your pants are falling down off your butt!" Translation: "Baby, you are slimming down! This is what we'd like to hear. This especially holds true if the man is dieting and or hitting the gym. We as men need to be reassured that we are sexy from time to time, especially if the man is giving a valid effort. The last thing a woman wants to hear is another woman complimenting her man. Ladies compliment your man, and every other woman is giving him a second opinion.

The biggest problem with single men impressing women is debt. Men will almost do anything financially to enhance his chances of landing that perfect 10. He'll trade his auto in for the next big trendy truck, which he can't afford. He'll buy $500 suits, $500 shoes, $50 cologne, and drink the finest wine/champagne all to impress a woman.

Still, that's not enough because he's only scratching the surface. A woman on the other hand won't do such a thing. She may buy an expensive dress on Friday for a date. She'll take better care of that dress than the store ever will. She'll strategically tuck away the price tags from site so that her date only notices every curve and cleavage of her body. The challenge for her is to only slow dance or dance so cute that she won't drop a bead of sweat. After a night of dinner and dancing she'll hang the dress and ferment it with febreeze just to return it to the store and say "Refund Please".

CHAPTER 3

Brides of Frankenstein

M EN ALWAYS KNOW what they want, unfortunately it's scattered about. If Dick Dynamite had a choice to build perfect women he would. She would look like Halle Berry. She'd have the lips of Angelina Jolie and Kirstie Alley eyes. The knowledge of Barbara Walters and Dr. Ruth combined. She has the body of Lisa Ray from Playa's Club. Then have a sense of humor like a Queen of Comedy. She has the confidence of an achiever. Exude pure innocence like a Catholic School girl, yet talented as Porn Star Vanessa Del Rio dressed like Wonder Woman. She would have to be as supportive as Hillary Clinton. Cook, clean and fix things like Martha Stewart. Lastly, goal oriented and financially sound as Oprah. You Go Girls! **THIS IS WHAT MEN REALLY WANT!** It's not much to ask. Men just have to figure out how to encourage women in the areas they're lacking. Until then, Dick Dynamite has a roster of several ladies whom satisfy him one way or another.

When building a Bride of Frankenstein, a man will gather many parts of a woman and piece them together according to his liking. Men want the total package, no matter what we tell you. We want it all. The truth is, we have it all until marriage occurs. We want a girl whom is in touch with reality but can fulfill our every sexual fantasy. Men want an intelligent girl with common sense. Dick needs a woman who can cook beyond the Hamburger Helper Recipe. She can also heat up a bedroom. Did I mention sex? We want a woman with drive, goals, and a dream. She must also be fit according to our body preference. Why settle for less. Did I mention properly administered oral sex to completion? Cheek and Tongue, Head and Shoulders, Bob and Weave, you get the message.

A bachelor will conquer several types of women in his lifetime in order to fulfill his needs while searching for what he thinks he wants. Theses Brides of Frankenstein are as follows: 1. Ole Faithful, 2. A Project Chic, 3. Frigid Francine, 4. White Chocolate, 5. Daddy's Lil Girl, 6. Kinky Caroline, 7. Felitia Freakright, and finally no.8, The Queen Bee. Each woman represents a chapter in a mans' life whom he'll carry a part of her with him his entire life. Unfortunately, that can enhance or hinder any future marital commitments.

Ole Faithful is usually Dick's first love. She tries her best to teach him love and he adheres, until something better comes along. Ole Faithful has the opportunity to be his first, or possibly take her virginity. Either way there's an ultimate sacrifice. She's usually more in love with him, than him loving her. If sex is involved, it's likely that the man is infatuated, and just loves the convenient sex. However, this doesn't apply to every man. This relationship starts with experiencing oral sex, anal sex, romance, and sometime genuine puppy love. Ole Faithful is very stern about monogamy in the relationship. She's definitely wifely material. Dick has no intention of cheating on his girlfriend but is constantly being introduced to friendly female beings. A few years go by, and Dick begins to go limp in the relationship. He feels crowded, curious about other ladies, and makes the crucial decision in staging a non-verbal breakup. This happens during the late teen years well into the early twenties. Now that Dick has ventured off to college or the Service, he will meet and marinate many women. Thus done unintentionally, forgetting Ole Faithful. There are so many women, so little time. Dick will begin to erect himself from Ole Faithful by comparing every woman he encounters to his now Ex-woman, Ole Faithful. Sadly, she served as his rock, teacher of love, romance, cultivation, and lastly the undeserving Door Mat. Dick's actions are unintentional but natural in his own mind. The saddest part of the whole ordeal is her broken heart and the disappointment to Dick's mom for dogging a wholesome young lady. Dick has just violated one of the three good women he will encounter in his life. Strike one!

Project Chic: Her title has nothing to do with her geographical location, but her state of mind. She's ghetto fabulous, hood like, Pimp stress, flamboyant, fashionable, sexual and dominant. Her only down fall is that she has short-term goals and concentrates on her body and looks to get what she wants from men. Here comes Dick, totally naïve to her agenda. Dick falls for her hook, line, and sinker after a night of dirty dancing and followed by a one-night stand. This one night stands escalates into frequent 3am Booty calls. The Project Chic totally understands Dick and wants no serious ties because she's a party girl. And Dick likes to party. Dick and this Chic have mutual respect for one another by keeping it superficial and sexual. The biggest problem Dick encounters with the Project Chic is when he wants to make a Booty Call and she has no one to keep her 7 kids, all by 4 different daddies. It usually gets sticky when one of the kids father pop up during your Booty Call, or before. Dick is only temporarily upset, but understands the rules. He'll wait until his time again. Rather it's a day or several weeks. It usually gets tricky when she requests a little financial help. Dick makes a quick decision to provide some monetary support so that he can continue to stop by late nights and violate every hole in her body without confrontation and limitations. Her sex is so good that it's dangerous. Dick will still stop by her house anyway for late night romp because it just increases sexual intensity. Dick puts his life on the line many times just to experience the recoil of her thrusting rear end during rigid butt slapping sex. POW! All while she's yelling, "Dick Dynamite make me bust! Make me bust! And when she does, it's like putting Niagara Falls inside a Dixie Cup. The Project Chic has Dick's number, and she knows how to pull it, when she wants something.

Frigid Francine: Still not satisfied, Dick is venturing off to fulfill more emptiness. He now befriends Frigid Francine. You know the type; she looks like a hot mamma, but her libido is like a Klondike bar. She's the sexy librarian, yet still wholesome. Francine almost has it all. She's independent, career oriented, grounded financially, good housekeeper, great cook, plus she has no kids. She claims she doesn't need a man. Truth is she can't keep a man due to her being violated in a rape early in life. Francine has some serious underlying issues that Dick becomes aware of after waiting 1 year before she had intercourse with him. Dick patiently waited until she was ready with no rush and no commitment. Francine is a possible candidate for commitment and marriage. Thus far, the picture looks perfect until the sex occurs. For starters, Francine doesn't mow her lawn too often in her southern regions. She looks like she giving birth to twins: Buckwheat and Don King. I guess if you don't get that many visitors, there's no need for a pathway. Secondly, Dick finds her clueless to how to receive his manhood and let alone thrust back. Dick uses every possible way of four play to relax Francine. When the sex begins, he wishes it was over. Dick fakes an orgasm just to stop from being turned off. Dick would probably have better sex at the local morgue. At least he'd probably get some involuntary movement. She's the type that only wants oral sex performed on her. She doesn't return the favor. Then she rolls over and falls asleep to awake like nothing happened. Meanwhile, Dick is left with a crusty face similar to a glazed donut and a pair of blue balls. Besides Francine being sexually inadequate and selfish, she's a nice person. Somehow Francine makes the cut by not being thrown away to the dogs. Dick will keep Francine as a plutonic friend. He enjoys her conversation, and respects her as a person. Dick will usually call on Francine as a showpiece for dinner parties and social affairs because she's groomed in upper class. Unfortunately, Francine usually falls for the wrong guys whom need a dominant woman. She's a "Repair Woman", she dates drug addicts and feel she can make them sober. She also dates felons and feel she can change them for the better. Dick notices this and decides to move on but keeps limited contact with Francine just to be cordial. I guess needy people need needy people.

White Chocolate: Every since slavery, mixed relationships have been cultural taboo. Most folks view Jungle Fever as empowerment, infiltration, sellouts, rebellious, and sometimes love. Truth of the matter, Dick is seeking a sexual adventure. There is a Dick in every race whom wants to test the racial boundaries and verify all sexual myths. The White Chocolate theory is that Black men tend to settle for white women once they reach a certain status in life. I honestly indulged in White Chocolate in the past and it was a matter of choice and the woman's personality. After conversing with several Black men on the topic, I found a common answer. Plain and simple, these brothers claimed that White Chocolate were more attentive to their needs. These men had an opportunity to be spoiled, instead of always doing the spoiling. They also agreed that black women put to much stress on them to provide for her needs only. They also claimed that White Chocolate was more in tune with their sexuality with no inhibitions. Some men even claimed that White Chocolate was better skilled in oral sex. Just the thought of these women enjoying giving their man some great head, made it easier for them to want to fulfill all her sexual needs. These White Chocoladites preferred black men for many reasons. The first reason was that they were both somehow subservient to the white man. The black man would actually listen to her ideas and thoughts. Secondly, black men are very confident in their sexual delivery making sure to get the job done, no matter how long it takes. The third and most prevalent was the larger penis size, and the ability to fill her vagina with orgasmic pleasure. These Black men felt no pressure and no stress in the relationship. However, there is a flipside. Some black men will date the sloppy, fat, nasty, white chocolate he can find. And he is so proud of his accomplishment. Not all interracial couples are targeted as sexual relationship. There are some black men whom are married to White Chocolate and love them dearly because she is a supportive Back Bone. Society just has to adjust to that fact and so do black women.

Black Beauty: You've seen her on an ordinary white mans arm. She's probably the finest black woman you've ever seen. What's good for the goose is good for the gander. However black men tend to take a white man dating a black beauty as stealing the mothers of the future and diluting the black race. White men have told me that black women are misunderstood, and only want attention. These White men love to spoil their black beauties. Many times these White men take the passive role in the relationship. White men see the Black Beauty as sassy, exotic, controlling and desires her juicy lips and big butt. Black women claim that they feel more secure with someone whom can meet their every demand. These white men also claim that White women can be too needy, and desire too much sex. My discussion with The Black Beauties was rather shocking. These black beauties claim that white men are more attentive to their needs emotionally and financially. Also, that some black men are intimidated with their beauty and independence. Many of nights they have been alone because black men assume they are already taken. These Black Beauties claimed white men were better skilled with the tips of their tongues during clitoral stimulations. Somewhere, a black man is upset because his black beauty thinks he's orally challenged. Honestly, it's all stereotypes.

As you see, Dick has no boundaries of the female gender. Dick thinks with both heads and concluded a general theory that all women are made the same.

Daddy Little Girl: When Dick encounters this woman, he's going to be constantly judged and challenged. Every man, Daddy Little Girl encounters is doomed from the start of the relationship. Dick doesn't have a chance to win this woman over completely because she's always seeking her dad's approval. No man is right in Daddy's eyes. She usually likes things done her way or no way. She can be very opinionated, mostly at the wrong times. Sexually, she's the aggressor but gratifying. She thinks like a man, and therefore she can sleep around with no shame. Dick views her as a hot chick with balls bigger than his. She's a threat to man ego because she is competitive in womanpower. However, her father taught her well about giving a man respect in the manner he deserves it. You'll have to earn her respect. These women usually make good wives, once a man has conquered her Daddy's checklist. She's so head strong that she's not the trustworthiest person in a relationship. Truth of the matter, her man is really her dad. She has the ability to use men for sex until she finds someone like her dear old dad.

Kinky Caroline: She is Dick sex goddess and she very much enjoys sex. She's usually an older woman whom is divorced or never married. She's very high maintenance, successful and could be labeled as a sugar mamma. Caroline only calls when she wants sex. When Dick arrives there's no talking just humping. Only time Dick mouth is allowed to move is when he's licking her like a stamp. She has no sexual hang ups and tells Dick exactly how to make her cum, again and again. She's very freaky! She likes for a man to place a vibrator in all orifices at full throttle while he slowly lick her clitoris in circular motions while she explodes. All while she looks him deep in the eyes. That's just fore play. She likes for sex to be hard thrusting and deep penetrating. She likes it so deep that she wants your testicles visiting her ovaries up close and personal. Dick usually bends her and twist her anyway possible and she cums without a hitch. Dick usually bangs it so hard that you can hear the thumping of their pelvic bones. This result is painful pleasure. She never ever complains. Kinky Caroline has many sex toys that she teaches Dick to use on her by eliminating the toy intimidation. She's a very unselfish lover whom likes to do the rise and fall of the penile tower. She supplies Dick with multiple oral orgasms by making him rise and fall then rise again, then fall and rise. She drains him to the point of dehydration. Several hours later of marathon sex, she indulges in general conversation to end his dismissal until next time. Every episode is a sexual lesson to be learned and later taught to another lover. She's the woman of Dicks dream but twice his age.

Felitia Freakright: She's the devil in drag posing as a nymphomaniac. She's the girl mother warned you about. She's the woman that is a threat to every wife or fiancé. She so sexy that you know she's trouble. She poses as a good girl with bad intentions. She could make a gay man straight, and send a preacher to hell. Everyman is vulnerable to Felitia. Her Game is so elusive and deceptive that she'll have Dick convinced he could do anything. She feels so right, but Ooooh so wrong. She targets married men or men in relationships. She doesn't want her own man, because it's too much of an attachment. When she's tired of men she switches to lesbians for security and heightened pleasure. Dick is only a pawn to her many challenges for conquering men. Her detached relationship probably extends from a sour relationship with her dad. Felitia can cook, clean, knows sports, financially secure, good sense of humor, and educated. When it comes to sex, she masturbates three times a day with porn or vibrators. She's insatiable. She likes being gang banged; all while she has her face plunged deep into a lesbian lover wetness hoping for an orchestrated group orgasm. Outside the bedroom, she's a good-hearted person whom is in denial about her life. She's very vindictive and wants everyone to feel the pain she's endured in her lifetime. She punishes men with sexual immorality and damnation. She's has no conscious. She's the best woman to ever share intimacy with because she truly doesn't need a man. But she's the last chosen because, of her carefree ways. She's an untamed stallion. Sexually, she may be a dream come true. Mentally, she's hell on wheels. She's addictive. She plays a deadly game. She plays for souls. When Dick sees this woman, he should go the other way.

However, the little head will do most of the talking, thinking and get the big head in trouble. She neutralizes all womanizers.

The Queen Bee: She is Heaven Sent by God above. Hopefully, she's a virgin and Christian. Therefore, Dick Dynamite has to change his negative ways in order to land this angelic creature. She is usually found when Dick at least expects her. The Queen Bee will discover her king. Believe it or not, every man is seeking her but in the wrong places. When she is discovered, it will be no mistake. Most men know when they have spotted their wives to be from the first time they lay eyes upon her. When this occurs, there is nothing sexual about his observation. Dick will watch her graceful ways only to ensue a plan that will pave their paths to meet. If she is God sent, Dick doesn't have to worry about his game. Her entire persona is so different from every woman Dick has ever encountered, and this is all noticed before ever speaking to her. Somehow this beautiful blessing is placed delicately in his life. This fragile moment can cause a man to rehash his past womanizing behavior and turn from sinner to saint. During his courtship, they'll spend long romantic evenings doing much of nothing but all of everything. The evening doesn't end there, it continues with five-hour phone conversations. These phone conversations are so in depth, Dick can't recall the topics. It just makes him feel loved. The phone call usually ends with Dick saying, "Good night, you hang up first". The Queen Bee saying, "No, You hang up first". Finally after several hours the conversation ends to awake with minimal sleep. Depending on Dick's age and status in life, he'll make a private decision that this woman is "The One". There's no need to look further. The funny part about this whole situation is Dick's friends pick up on his vibe of loving this woman. Single men tend to share sexual war stories about their romps in the hay. Those days are over when the Queen Bee comes in his life. Dick's friends notice a change in his behavior. The first change is he no longer feels a need to bed other women. He also won't share intimate details about their relationship. Nor will he make any disrespectful comments or allow any to be directed at his Queen. There comes a day in many men life, when he awakes and decides he's bored with meaningless relationships. He doesn't want to be a pimp, playboy or Sex Toy. Dick realizes that all along that these women he dealt with weren't the fools, he was. He finally realized that when a man distributes his effort and body to several women simultaneously, he has spread himself thin.

He is now so thin that he's transparent and sees himself for what he really is, a loathing man. He reminisces over his past attempts to satisfy every woman's need physically and sometimes mentally. He no longer has to juggle women during Christmas Holidays so that they won't feel alone. He no longer has to plot a time schedule for the impossible "New Years Eve" commitment. Women figure, if you spend New Years Eve with them at the stroke of Mid Night, then it's a possibility that you are only focused on her. Men need to focus on themselves first by setting priorities and not breaking promises. Dick now has the difficult task of breaking off each relationship one by one in a timely manner. This is a very difficult process to complete because Dick has engulfed himself so deep in each woman that she feels they have a connection. Truthfully, the only connection is casual sex and meaningless favors. Now that Dick Dynamite has begun to cut his ties to the other distractions, he'll patiently await the Queen Bee grace period for intimacy. Most men will wait 90 days up to 1 year. Ladies don't be fooled; he's waiting with you but probably not elsewhere. However, I could be wrong. Ladies stick to your guns; he'll respect you more in the long run. What is meant to be is meant to be. Ladies don't ruin the situation by rushing the man. This is a new found territory for a dog; he's sniffing the grounds to see how many others have been there, and who poses a threat. Meanwhile, continue to order your Bridal magazines but don't force it down his throat. Dick will let you know when he is ready, and not before then. Unfortunately, most women are impatient with mans decision making process thus accusing him of fearing commitment. Truly sweetheart, you have no idea what this man is experiencing. If the woman applies too much pressure, there's a chance that this man will retreat back to his old ways. Be careful and patient. Women of today are more confident and should be more assertive in asking the man of his hand in marriage. Many women are starting to take untraditional measures of landing her Mr. Right. There is absolutely nothing wrong with showing a man his worth. She should approach the engagement by getting down and proposing on both her knees. This method isn't sexual, symbolic, or subservient, it just shows that she is confident in her approach of wanting to please and marry her man. These are the types of things that need to occur if women claim they are our equals. I totally support women in taking the initiative in doing whatever they feel. If you snooze, you lose! When the Queen Bee has won Dick Dynamites heart and proved her worthiness, he will submit for love and love only. Hopefully he won't submit for entrapment or guilt of what has transpired in the relationship; such as guilt in prolonging the wedding over several changed wedding dates or babies out of wedlock. Dick should do it for genuine love first, and everything else will fall into place. The newest downfall of choosing a bride is convincing her to take your last name in marriage. A feminist movement has influenced many new brides to opt for keeping her last name with a hyphen, or adding his last name behind her maiden name. That's absolute non-sense. She has just administered the first argument and unspoken separation. Men whom allow this disrespect have already set the stage for him to be played like a punk. Any woman, who doesn't wants to solely take on her husband name, has something to hide. She can't be trusted. Most women keep the maiden name with the new name, which allows her to hold two identities. Mostly the identity scam is used in keeping her credit score separate from his, as well as hidden finances, and property. It's basically the woman's version of a prenuptial agreement. Men need to wise up and walk away when his bride-to-be refuses to take his last name. If the groom name is not good enough for the bride, then she is not good enough to be his wife. She's already dodging her wifely duties. Women constantly complain that they want a man to charm them, pamper them, and console them. But she will refuse the thing that's most important in marriage, the validation of being identified as a married couple instead of a Law Firm; Mr. & Mrs. (Smith-Jones and Jones). No Hyphens Gentlemen!

CHAPTER 4

Thee Bachelor Funeral (Wedding Day)

NO ONE TO TOUCH
NO LATE NIGHT LOVE MAKING AND WHISPERING
NO COLD FEET UPON MY LEGS
NO NAILS RUNNING DOWN MY CHEST
NO WARM BODY PRESSED AGAINST MINE
NO PLAN MAKING FOR TOMMORROW
NO ONE TO HOG ALL THE COVERS
AND NO ONE TAKING DEEP BREATHS IN THEIR SLEEP
AND JUST A SLIGHT BREATH TOUCH MY NOSE

By Rhythm of Life

THIS EVENT LEADING up to the death of a bachelor can be a traumatizing experience that often leaves paranoid thoughts of the past and the future colliding. We like to call these, "cold feet". All of a sudden Dick tries to convince himself that he reacted on an impulse when requesting the Queen Bee hand in marriage. Truthfully he did the right thing, but he often wonders how he got to this point. The most prevalent thoughts that fill his mind are losing his friends, whom he has known longer than his future wife. He also realizes that he will have to make love with the same woman time after time. Dick can deal with seeing his friends occasionally, but it's going to be difficult for him to accept bedding one woman for the rest of his life.

Therefore, Dick Dynamite is literally giving up his name and ranking only to be placed in the Players Hall of Fame with mere memories. Most men have an opportunity to unleash the beast at the Bachelor party. No matter what you've done in your bachelor life, the bachelor party makes you legendary.

I recall my own bachelor party and it was legendary indeed. However, it started off slow and tragic. A friend of the family brought over two crack head dancers, in which one had front teeth missing. The other had a gunshot wound in her breast that looked like a third nipple. The worst part was, they were both bald headed and trying to sew each other hair weave in at the same time, while 30 drunk and horny onlookers booed. Fortunately for me, the week before, several of my buddies and I hit all the upscale strip clubs with invites for the dancers to come and perform. It was just something we did for fun. I'm glad we chose that tactic because we had charged guys $20 for all you can eat and all the alcohol you can drink. The party started at 10 pm. I kicked the crack head strippers out by 11pm. About 11:30 pm a few chunky girls waddled in with all their teeth and no bullet wounds. That calmed the guys down severely. When the clock struck 12 midnight, about 30 of the finest female dancers showed up in garters, camisoles, and thongs under trench coats. When we opened the door, it took about 10 minutes before we could gather them in the house. The guys went nuts. The DJ played every Booty Shaker song ever made. Every single person at that party was high, drunk, getting laid or all of the above. The aroma was a mixture of booty, Seasoning Salt, and weed. Dudes were totally out of order. One friend of ours poured straight Hennessey down a dancer's kit-kat, thus creating a fountain into his glass. She enjoyed it at first, and then she jumped screaming in sheer pain from the alcohol scorching her insides.

Then we got a lesbian "Strap-on" show, with an aggressive stripper banging the other girls brains out which brought them to tearful orgasms. Next thing you know guys started disappearing into different rooms, some 2 and 3 couples at a time. I enjoyed a lap dance.

I was never known as a drinker. I had drank so much, I feared I would miss the wedding the next day. I had one of my buddies' get me home about 4am. I staggered around the house in prepping my tuxedo and other garments for the wedding that was less than 12 hrs away. I rested about 90 minutes to sober up, shower, and headed to the church at 6am. I slept from 6 a.m. in front of the church in my car until about 4 pm to be awakened by the preacher saying "its show time". As I attempted to dress my self, I realized I was still hung over from the night before, and it only got worse. It was hot as hell that day. I was sweating like a runaway slave following Harriet Tubman. By the time I got to the altar, my tuxedo was completely sweated out. I had brought a towel, but that was drenched. My "wife to be" was late. I was ready to pass out. My Dad and uncles had to console me because I look faint. I was dehydrated and nauseated. Finally the bride showed up and I was done. It's amazing that I made it through the service. The cold feet really started to kick in, "I kept saying to myself, just pass out and maybe we'll post pone it." Then the pastor asked if I was going to be all right. I told him you just make it quick. Even though I took a shower before the service, my pores smelled like a brewery. At that point, the pastor already announced for better or for worse. My point in telling my story is men have a different view on the marriage process. We view it as our end to what we once represented. The bachelor party is just an outlandish event for the grooms buddies to have fun one last time. The party is truly for the groomsmen. The girls are all meant for his friends as a gift saying; "I'm leaving now you guys, take it from here." The groom trades in the wingman status to become the "The Gipper". The groom has done everything for his friends and himself until this point. Actually the Bachelor Party is the male high point in the marital process.

Women view the marital process as tedious, timely, and down right stressful. We as men want no parts of that process. Therefore we just agree on the colors chosen, patterns selected, caterers and willing to fork over the money with no arguments. The groom can ultimately do everything the bride requests and she'll feel you're leaving all the plans up to her. Honestly, she doesn't value your opinion because this is something that she, her mom, aunts, and grandma has mentally planned since she was a little girl. She finally got her "Knight in Shinning Armor". A mans job is to just show up, be on time, and look happy. Word of advice ladies, don't seek our opinion when you really don't value our thought process of the wedding plans. They only use a man decision when they want to decide to be rid something. Women view this day, as their Cinderella story and nothing should ruin that moment. Most men are looking to get past all the planning and stress so they may start their new lives together. Some women are more in love with the idea of marriage, rather than the person their actually marrying. Marriage is more complex than that. It's so complex that you need counseling before the marriage to ensure you're compatible. Plus you'll need a license, a witness, and a promise to God. Sometimes you'll need counseling during marriage and may even seek counseling to terminate the marriage. There's no room for screw-ups. These are all the ideas the man is thinking about during the whole planning process. Men are hoping that we can hold it together, and not how many layers of cake to order.

Weddings and Funerals have many similarities. Women cry heavily at weddings and funerals. There are usually six groomsmen or Paul Bearers at the altar firmly supporting you so you won't hit the floor. The same Groomsman or Paul Bearers make sure that you get to the church early so that people can view you in disbelief. Ironically, your peers come to view the shell of a fun loving person whom will be no more. Finally, when departing the church, people are either throwing rice or dirt at the last suit you'll ever wear. Either way it goes, Dick Dynamites life as he once knew it is over. He is reincarnated as Mr. Richard Was.

Managing your wife

Before every man settles down he needs to know the seven categories of wives he will possibly endure. For better or for worse, he will encounter one of the seven women. The seven wife types are typical in our society. Ask any married man, and he'll tell you which characters are his wife. I will list these wives from 1 to 7 with their pro's and cons, and possible resolutions to get what you want and need.

1. **The Cling-On:** She's the wife that barely allows her husband any space and believes that every available moment of his spare time should be spent with her. When she's not with him, she's constantly calling the cell phone, paging, or calling ahead to see if he has arrived. She's very insecure from possible abandonment issues, lack of trust, and or guilt from her own infidelity. She's very tactful in watching her husband without him even realizing it. She'll always send the kids to accompany the husband wherever he goes. The husband also being the good father figures he's just spending time with his kids. Sadly, everyone around him realizes what's taking place, except for him. His entire existence is devoted to work, family, spouse, kids, sleeping and paying bills. Notice, I never mentioned personal time. He has no time for himself. This husband is a prime candidate for an affair because he's being smothered. He also feels he's not trusted and should indulge what the wife already expects him of doing. Men beware of this woman because she is killing you softly! It's one thing to give up your life in marriage, but never negotiate your personality. This is a small step of when the wife is trying to change the man. I blame those husbands whom are in this predicament because it's not mandatory. The man must stand up tell his wife that she is suffocating him and he needs to breathe in his personal life. She may be resentful for a while but the more you stress that point, she'll grow respectful of your wishes. The man with a peace of mind is a whole man. (**The Cling-on** is formerly **Ole Faithful**).

2. **The Corporate B!tch:** She's the hardest one to crack. In most cases she has been brainwashed by her employer to believe she can do anything and everything better than male co-workers. This wife is also influenced by her peers and family to push beyond reasonable expectations, usually at her husbands expense. She is the mate procrastinating on a family because of her career. The corporate world has contaminated her mind so, that she has become mentally child barren. The Corporate B!tch brings her work home and tries to run the home like her office. She has become a shell of a woman. She's a man masquerading in a woman's body. She thinks like a man, acts like a man, and wants to converse or argue like a man. She needs to be put in her place. The husband in this situation should support his business minded wife but not be unappreciated. Truth of the matter, she'll respect and appreciate her boss more than her husband. Why? Because she believes her job supports her more mentally and financially than the husband. There's also the flipside to this wife type. She may have once been a happy home maker and decided she wanted more. Maybe she couldn't deal with the kids and the lifestyle of keeping a good home. She took the same energy to work and became the "Company Man". The Corporate

B!tch is the most selfish out of the seven wives in every aspect of her life becomes business from a dinner date to sex. Don't even discuss sex! If you can't email her a "Nooner" or fax it, forget it! When she does decide to have sex with the husband, he'll get a memo. The memo will specify when, where, why, how, and how long. Now the husband has to clear his calendar for this briefing, and I do mean brief. Men if you encounter this wife, you have to speak her language. Make sure she understands at work she's the boss. When she's home, you're always the boss. She wants to be directed and she's wants to be spoiled, and then manhandled. Husbands need to be firm but fair. Most of all never let your bed turn into her office. Delegate her time schedule to fit you in where you belong. She'll thank you later. If any husband with this type of wife turns wussy, he's a shredded document. You have to be more than a paper weight with her, because those same male co-workers she's spending time with will spark her interest. Next thing you know, she's passed you a virus from some guy downloading on her hard drive. This is not the time for a floppy disk. (**The Corporate B!tch** is formerly **Daddy's Little Girl**, or **Kinky Caroline**).

3. **The Happy Homemaker:** She's perfect! She cooks, cleans, tend the kids, and fixes things. She's your very own Martha Stewart. She's the way God intended it to be. Unfortunately, she's a rarity. She waits on her man hand and foot. She respects her husband decision and never second guesses him. She makes the husband life a dream come true. The husband should appreciate this woman wholeheartedly. The only downfall with this wife type, she has the tendency to gain excessive weight. I advise husbands to implement a workout schedule for the wife when she can get out the house 3 times a week. Just be sure she's working out at the gym and not some hotel. The husband should never turn down her wishes to buying something special for herself. She must always be romanced, to the extreme. He should always make her feel like a queen, no matter what. After all, she makes the husband feels like a King. (**The Happy Homemaker** is formerly **Ole Faithful**)

4. **Mrs. Ever Ready:** She's a sexual wildcat! She'll do it any time, any place, any position. She has a checkered past of experimentation with males and females. This husband is blessed with a curse because at any given time she may have an insatiable appetite for fish or beef. You may not be invited! She'll usually keep her habits under wraps. This type of wife can make a man insecure because she has no limits. This is the type of wife that will do her dirt right under his nose and he won't smell a thing. If you have this type of wife, I would strongly suggest **not** working a mid-night shift, **ever!** You can trust her, but you'll have to watch her. Everyman wants his wife to be a woman in public, and a freak in the bedroom. Some wives just need to be reminded that the freak clause is "Exclusive to the husband". She's the perfect "Swingers Wife" for the "Swingers type". Good luck with this one hubby. You got your work

cut out! Momma told you not to marry that girl! (**Mrs. Ever Ready** is formerly **Felitia Freakright**).

5.   **The Back Bone:** She's down for her husband, no matter what. She works, cooks, cleans, has great sex, respect her man to the utmost. She knows her place but will not allow her man to disrespect her. She's a franchise player. She was cultivated from birth by her family on how to treat a man. The way she loves, allows her access to any and everything she desires. It's all respect! Respect your husband and you can expect the best! This woman is so good to her husband, that if she died, they'd hold a double funeral just so he can be with her. She's irreplaceable. She is what Eve was supposed to be to Adam. She completes this husband. She caters to him, respects him, love him, sexually gratifies him, and financially assisting him is what makes "The Back Bone". Any husband that screws up a marriage with this wife type deserves to die alone. She is hand crafted by God. Pure perfection can't be altered or disrespected. (**The Back Bone** is formerly known as **The Queen Bee** or **White Chocolate**).

6.   **The Church Lady:** She's spiritually sound and quotes the Bible at random. She attends church and Bible study on a regular basis. She's a good wife and tends to her wifely duties. Her downfall, she's a hypocrite. She raises hell all week just to go to church and bleach away her sins. She's an instigator, gossip queen, and judgmental of peers. This wife type is seen as nosy and unbearable. The husband is usually hen-pecked and forced to hear about others business. The best resolution to this wife is to tell her to practice what she preaches. She needs to concentrate her energy of handling issues within her own home. The husband needs to spend more time with his wife because she probably indulges out of boredom. If the hubby gives her the business in more ways than one, maybe she'll mind her own. She needs a hobby. Most of all, hubby should attend church with her on a regular basis. She's a good soul with a busy body. Lastly, she's a beautiful woman with sexual hang ups which frustrates her attentive husband. (**The Church Lady** is formerly **Frigid Francine**).

7.   **The Material Girl:** This wife is a total flake and the husbands know it! She's very high maintenance and seeks the finest things in life. The word **work** is a bad word to her. Her money is her money, and the husband money is hers also. She is driven by money, and keeping up with The Jones's. This wife has been groomed to take advantage of men since the day she was born. She was groomed by greedy aunts, and or a bitter mother whom past lovers did them wrong. They usually grow materialistic in their teens by chasing the guy with the nicest car or who spends the most money. Usually these women can be cold hearted toward a man whom has nothing to offer her. God forbid a man marries this type of woman and then fall on hard times. He'll see the truth about his wife. The Material Girl spends money with no countenance. She'll run up credit cards even after hubby cut up the Visa. She's so dedicated to

shopping, she memorizes the card numbers. The material girl is destined to marry a pro athlete or entertainer. God help that man if he has a career ending injury or fall gravely ill. If he dies, she's hit the Jackpot. It's all about her and the money. The best advice I can give to any man whom thinking of marrying a Material Girl is, "DON'T!" Men know in advance that his future wife is a gold digger, especially if she's out his league. However, if his league is the NBA, she'll play him. Marriage with these women is prioritizing money over looks, money over sex, and money over poverty. The Material Girl is addicted to men with power. No Power, No Pu$$y! Where's is the Love? (**The Material Girl** is formerly known as **The Black Beauty** or **The Project Chic**).

CHAPTER 5

Let the marriage games begin!

MARRIAGE CAN BE a hypocritical unsolved mystery that couples seek an answer to. Only God knows the resolution. Gods plan for marriage is for couples to be committed to one another and worship him in union. Even the nearest to perfect marriages fall short of Gods glory. There was a time when 50% of all marriages were doomed for divorce. Recent polls show 2 out of 3 marriages end in divorce. These stats make you honestly wonder why people invest in love to end up broke financially and in spirit. God never fails, but marriages do every day. I consider myself a God fearing man but I become distraught in understanding the outline of marriage. I respect Our Heavenly Fathers directions on marriage, but I often wonder what it would be like if God had a wife. It would have probably taken 6 years to create the world instead of six days. Mrs. God would have accused God of taking to much time on that "Human Life" project, only to be scrapped. The Bible clearly states the do's and don't, but there is no guideline on how to react in problem marriages. Of course there's counseling, but the counselor doesn't walk in your shoes. I have no intentions of appearing blasphemous but I feel like God didn't give the male gender enough knowledge on females when it comes to their wants. And they want everything. Men basically learn how to be a husband by trial and error. I have never met a man whom said he was taught to be a good husband by his father. Men are only given advice in which he has to use at his discretion. What might work in another man's house won't work in yours. My point, marriage would be more enjoyable if women said what they needed instead of making men read their minds. However, they have no problem sharing their ideas or concerns with another woman. They call us stupid? Ladies clue us in on what you want, or get ignored. A husband walks around in a daze thinking his wife is problem free. The wife usually takes her time by allowing her complaint to fester into a time bomb for the hubby. She'll unload the bomb right before an intimate moment. That is so predictable and inappropriate.

After about 6 months of marriage, the warranty wears off. Say good-bye to the frequent sex. No more "Nooners", no "Morning Eye Openers" or Midnight Mating". The realization of marriage settles upon a couple. The woman finds her need of cuddling is more important than sex. This can be a problem for Richard Was (Formerly Dick Dynamite). Richard may find himself putting on weight due to the comfort zone of home cooked meals and lack of exercise. Richard may no longer act as a gentleman pursuing chivalry. He used to open every mall door for his Queen B. Now she's lucky if the door doesn't knock a hole in her head after he's already entered first. Before marriage, Richard would open his queens car door in rain, sleet or snow. Now he only opens her door on Birthdays, Church outings, or infrequent dates. When he does actually open and closes her car door, he usually slams her leg by a planned mistake. Quickly replying, "I'm sorry!" Truth of the matter is, men tend to show all their best qualities in courting a woman just to achieve the status of possibly "sexing her". No husband can continue to get good loving without continual chivalry even if it's corny. Men have to continue to do all things in marriage that he did for his Queen in courtship if he wants to keep her. That means everything! That's the only part of Dick Dynamite that must remain alive. Ladies too, must do the same.

There was a time when Richard and his Queen would spend hours at a time talking on the phone about romantic nothings. Now when she calls, he tries to limit his conversations to no longer than 5 minutes due to a fear of being nagged. Richard used to tell her, "I Love you! You hang up first". Richard used to love the sound of the dial tone. Richard now ends conversations in conflicts, frustration, and avoidance. The Queen no longer cares who hangs up first; because the one who hears the dial tone now loses. What happened to the love? Another change that occurs is ownership of the utilities. If possible men, put the bills in your own name. Not your momma name. Women truly expect for the man to be the support system to all her needs, want and desires. If Richard doesn't meet her needs then, he'll be **meating his** own needs. Marriage is supposed to be a couple, in teamwork. Unfortunately, each gender role contributes to good sex only to decline and cancel out communication.

The biggest problem in marriage from time to time is managing a joint bank account. Joint accounts are where most arguments begin because no one wants to submit their money as one income in exchange for an allowance. Richard is likely to be the hesitant one to submit to the idea because of his wifes spending habits. A strange thing happens to women and money in a marriage. The woman tends to still spend her money, as if she is still single. Richard has to sacrifice his wardrobe, sleep and livelihood to keep them out of debt. Richard will usually have to work over-time, hustle on the side, and make cut backs just to stay above debt. Richard is slowing noticing his wife faults that he never knew existed. She's a shop-aholic. Plus she indulges in credit fraud by opening up credit cards in his name. Richard starts noticing that bills aren't being paid on time and funds are being switched around more the "3 Card Monty". Upon noticing this problem, Richard approaches his wife on this matter only to be told that the money was put on a past due bill from way back. It had to be paid before it was shut off. Richard is completely in the dark on the matter because the credit card bills are forwarded to her girlfriends, sister, or maybe even his mother-in-law. Everybody is in on the scam except for Richard. Women tend to use that loophole in the vows **"for richer or for poorer"**. Translated, that means the more money Richard makes, the more she can shop. The poorer becomes, the more he'll be in the dark. Women always have a secret stash, and surprisingly their husbands fund the transaction. A woman is always holding out the amount of money she's saving. She has been trained from a child to keep something for herself and never depend on a man. Men don't be naïve in thinking your wife or woman is broke. She probably has more money than you at any given time. She's just waiting for you to handle the finances with your money. Her money is her money, and your money is your money. Don't believe me, get in a bind and ask for her help and watch how fast she comes up with the money. Here is a classic example of how a man is constantly trying to keep a continual cash flow in his home to stay ahead of debt, but failed in the process. My sister-in-law recently set up a photo sessions with her mother and step-dad, her stepson, nephews, me (the brother-in-law), and her sisters. The photo was to appear in the Pastors Anniversary program, which was paid for by the women. This was a mandatory photo shoot. I guess my brother-in-law didn't get the memo. Needless to say, all hell broke loose by women snapping on the men that were present. My brother-in-law caused such a ruckus because his priorities were to make his money in his self employed business. I was basically left to fend for myself. I made the crucial mistake of asking where he was, and when would he arrive. Suddenly, tempers and attitudes flared from my sister-in-law so fast that she decided to exclude him from the photo. His excuse was valid, "I was making money." Amazingly the photo was beautiful, and seemed peaceful but that was hardly the case. Several weeks later, the photo arrives from the photographer with an obvious space between my sister-in-law and her stepson. Immediately my mother-in-law contacts her daughter complaining how my brother-in-law ruined this extensive family photo by not being present. My mother-in-law was insisting on having her way, she convinced her daughter that she wants a COMPLETE family photo. My sister-in-law later reveals at a Easter Dinner at my house that she was willing to pay Kinko's $60 to Cut, Paste, and Crop **her husbands image (from another photo)** into this portrait regardless of his absence. Damn! This brings new meaning to being somewhere you don't want to be! This proves every man's theory that **a woman will go to the extremes to get her way, whether you like it or not!** I have to give my sister-in-law props on her high tech tabloid creativity. My brother-in-law stated "Hell if I'd known she was going to place me at the scene of an alibi, I would have robbed a bank that day!" No pun intended, but "The kid stays in the picture!" I just hope this **high-tech henpecking** doesn't catch on because men will be appearing all over the world and don't own a Pass Port. Men heed this lesson when supporting your wife, or be subjected to meeting your clone with **finer resolution**. Men beware! If you don't do it for her, Kinko's will. And Kinko's will produce a good man at a dime a dozen! A woman's way of thinking has really gone beyond man primitive mind. Women, you win! Hands Down!

Many women complain that their husbands don't spend quality time with them. The Richards of the world are too busy working trying to keep the house from foreclosure and she's trying to get to the mall before closing. The Queens of the world need to step up their game and support the hubbies in his weekly plight to defeat that bully, Bill. The day that women recognize their inner strength is the day that she'll get everything she wants and Richard will see to that. A woman can turn a good man bad and make a bad man better. When the Queens of the world decide to use their powers for good, Richard can take on the world and win. Because now, Richard is fighting to keep his good thing until the day he dies.

When a man marries a woman, he marries her whole family. That includes the money grubbing members, the alcoholics, crack heads, the felons, snooty millionaires, and judge mental preachers. The stage is set and everybody is on the outside looking in to criticize. If most men take a good look at his future in-laws before marriage, he can see the future. Every family has a flaw; usually every man finds it but only to late. My advice is to attend all family activities before marriage and take a consensus of the women in attendance. If a man looks closely, he'll observe his Queens past, present and future. There are **3 stages**. The first is the **youth & beauty**. Youth & Beauty is my favorite because that's the look a man falls in love with. There's inner beauty as well as visual beauty. There was a time when all the women in her family looked glamorous and fit. As time changes, the next level is **Post baby vs. Midlife**. This is where most women fall completely apart with inner beauty and outer beauty. This is when the man takes notice of the women in the family whom are mother's 5yrs to 10yrs removed. If she's reminiscing over pictures in her hey day and saying her big stomach is baby fat from her 21 yr. old son, that maybe a Kodak moment into your Queens future. The only time a man feels a little weight is acceptable is when the woman has been petite all her life. It's then much appreciated, especially if the weight gain is in the right places. If Richard has married a **"Brick House"** and her mother and aunts look like **"Two Family Flats"** he may want to supervise his wife's construction so her butt doesn't grow a new room addition. There's a good chance his queen may become fat, if the mother and aunts are fat. Who say's you need a Crystal Ball, just stare in your female in-laws guts and butts and you'll see your wife's future. Let's hope I'm wrong, but I doubt it. The last stage is the **Senior Citizen vs. the Silver fox**. There's nothing sexier than a women whom has maintained her body, charm, sex appeal, and beauty at 50 yrs and beyond. That's dedication to herself and her husband. A man should still have a wife that's appealing, even in her golden years. Men in turn should do the same in making an effort to look desirous throughout their life of marriage.

A woman position stays the same in a marriage, but usually the man makes the personal adjustments over the years. In the midst of marriage, Richard must find a position of firmness and fairness without being outwitted by his wife. There's always a time when the Queen will challenge his manhood on sound decisions. There's a thin line between being hen-pecked and being a compromising hubby. Men always know the borders but women push the boundaries. It's hard to be firm and fair when you always come out to be the bad guy in front of peers and in-laws. The last thing Richard wants is to appear controlling. It's okay for a woman to be controlling and bossy but when a man does this, people speculate domestic abuse. Controlling and nagging are always double standards.

Richard has two options. The first is sticking to his guns and subjecting him to a possible wife strike. The second option, is allowing him to be disrespected and doubted every time. Richard needs to earn his wife respect by holding a strong position. If Richard retracts his plan, he is considered **"Hen-pecked"**. A Hen-Pecked man is worthless, useless, and should be sent out to pasture and shot. He is a misrepresentation of the male gender. He has no rights, no confidence, no balls and no authority. He often compromises his needs for the peace and approval from his wife. Even the strongest of studs can be broken like a horse. The only chance of avoiding Hen-pecking is acknowledging the behavior. Upon acknowledging her behavior, he must aggressively approach and cease her program. A nagging woman can make Richard feel as if he's suffocating. Nagging can be harmful to a woman's health. When a man is being nagged beyond toleration, he snaps. Snapping usually leads to verbal abuse, domestic abuse, death, and extra marital affairs.

Domestic Disputes!

When a man is angered, a wise woman would be smart to give him space. As of lately, some wives have developed more testosterone and challenge their husbands to fistfights. These treacherous women abuse the judicial system by posing psychological threats to the husband's authority, opinions and points of view with frequent visits from the police. These cowardly wives use the government and taxpayer's dollars to get a choke hold on her husband, while she gets her way. Many men are suffering loss of jobs and civil rights due to fraudulent police reports. **I don't condone any man beating his wife**, at all. But those women who choose to slap, push and point fingers along the husband's head, and then hail harsh words at his man hood, deserves to be put in check. My defense is for the husbands whom don't practice spousal abuse. However, they are often challenged and disrespected as the heads of their homes by aggressive wives. These men are great husbands whom go above and beyond the call of duty. These women need to stop calling Wolf! If a wife acts like she has a pair of balls, then she deserves to be kicked in the nuts! Bottom line, wives need to stay in line with head of the household, and stop physically and verbally disrespecting these men when she can't have her way. Women will learn that if they continue to jump in a husbands face with physical and verbal threats, they will continually be treated like a man. In other words ladies, how many lumps do you want? Once again, **I don't defend** the brute that kicks the dog, and physically or verbally abuse his family because he's having a bad day. Sadly, this mans actions though wrong may feel justified by the means. Men tend to operate on their own clock especially at home. The smartest thing a woman can do is allow her husband his personal time with plenty of space. Each gender should respect what one another are capable of doing. A woman reacts on emotion and will do all she can to make a man loose his cool to the point of being physical. A man will endure the minimal emotional trauma to his ego, and then it's time to hit something or someone. I strongly advise men to keep their hands to themselves or buy a punching bag. I advise women not to target his hot button, because his hot button can target you. Truthfully, just because he has never hit you, he's at least thought about it once or twice. Heated moments are very dangerous. Wives need to know when to back off, and men need to know when to restrain themselves. I'll make it simple for wives; just listen to your conscience. "If I say such and such and he's already mad, will this get me a fat lip?" Maybe! Maybe Not! Don't test his patience. Men don't listen to your ego! "Pow! Hit her right in the kisser!" Please don't slap her silly or attack her emotionally by saying something very cruel. **It's not worth it, retreat to your personal space and pray for guidance.** As we all know, a woman will get the last word even if she's spitting out her teeth as she saying them. Man must be the bigger individual and retreat to prayer and return for a quiet resolution. Wives must **learn to shut up** and not push the right buttons that will get their heads lumped. Sometimes silence is Golden, and blood is red. Badgering a man on any given wrong day is equivalent to asking her, "How many lumps do you want?" She too, must retreat in peace to a safe haven before any potential outbursts occur. In other words husbands and wives alike must use common sense. 1 Tim 2:11-13 (NIV) **A WOMAN SHOULD LEARN IN QUIETNESS AND FULL SUBMISSION. I DO NOT PERMIT A WOMAN TO TEACH OR TO HAVE AUTHORITY OVER A MAN; SHE MUST BE SILENT. FOR ADAM WAS FORMED FIRST, THEN EVE.**

Wives are always watching the clock and every moment seems to be the end of the world. Husbands will spend their marital lives working, sacrificing and subjection to humiliation from their employers to keep their Queens happy. Nothing angers Richard more than coming home from a hard day work to nonsense or a woman whom has to wait on her husband for everything. Men hate to be nagged about a preexisting situation already discussed. This holds true when the problem has already been assessed and in the process of resolution.

Mans Livelihood

The key to a man heart is through his livelihood, not his stomach. What is his livelihood? His livelihood is any recreation that makes him happy without his wife. It may be a hobby, activity, fishing, stamp collecting, playing the guitar or building model toys. Whatever it is, the wives need to leave them the hell alone. This is his place of peace and selfish happiness. He controls that domain without critics or nagging dragons.

Many people have **the wrong impression of marriage**. There's no such thing as a Happy Marriage. That's definitely an oxymoron. There's no white picket fence, no being bill free, and **no constant sex**. Many couples won't admit that it's not what they expected. Marriage is institution for building a family with values all while appearing as a hypocrite to your children based on your past. A man learns the truth about his wife when he marries. When a woman is single, she hides all the little annoying things and habits that have turned other men away and dumps them on you once married. Men have complained that their wives like to use the restroom with the door open no matter if she's peeing or taking a dump. Not mention holding a conversation at the same time with her hubby or friend by phone. When she was dating for the first year, the man never seen or smells her taking a dump. She would rather experience abdominal cramping before he knew she took a crap. That is so un-lady like and nasty. Then there are times when wives want to violate her husband's space while he's using the rest room by brushing her teeth, doing her hair or wanting to take a shower. Men are territorial, and we need our space, especially when sitting on the throne and reading the paper.

Other little quirks are the irritating sounds she makes with her throat whenever her sinuses are bothering her. It sounds like a pig and duck having sex in an echoed area. Imagine that. She never showed her hubby that when they were dating. The first time he views that; he thought she was having a fit. Lastly, other quirks include the sleep walking, talking in sleep, acting out dreams aka the Dream Actress, and the favorite "Sleeping Pooty" the pooter in denial. These are things men discuss and it drives us nuts when women constantly do them. Honestly, many men would have ran in a different direction if he had noticed these irritating issues early in the courtship.

Marriage is the longest running theatrical play known to mankind. The actual marriage is the stage for everyone to see, criticize and judge. The husband and wife are the characters whom from time to time, act like they're happy in front of their audience. Everything may appear perfect, but it's only superficial. These actors want their perception to actually become their reality. The perception is that they're so perfect and loving. However, back in the green room/ home, disagreements are unresolved. These actors put their differences aside to follow a happier script for their in-laws, co-workers, family and friends. Each performance receives critical acclaim for success by making others wish they were married or had a marriage like the actors before them. Every so often one of the actors publicly deviates from the agreed script and ventures into an angry improvisation also known as an argument. The audience will gasp in fear because that scene wasn't in the script. Marriage is a windowed showpiece that looks appealing from any avenue onlooker. However, people have no clue of the work a marriage takes to become or even seem polished. The bottom line, happily married is a mundane phrase a couple may use to convince themselves and others that it's not a death sentence. Actually, it's till death do you part.

Emotions are also a big part of marriage that comes easily for women. I would strongly advise any man to confide in a female marriage counselor or an older experienced married woman to display sensitivity. Sadly, women always are allowed to discuss their feelings and we must listen or be subjected to a strike. Men constantly battle their emotions vs. their egos. The emotions usually touch on the sensitive side of men, which delivers **Thee Uncomfortable Truth** to their mate. Women don't care to hear that her man has hurt feelings, or if he's offended, let alone depressed about something. Women see men as strong pillages that never breakdown or collapse. Men experience the same mental issues women embark, except we keep them to ourselves. Husbands' wish to discuss everything with their wives, but they fear they'll be patronized, ridiculed, and exploited for their feelings. Plus, men are secretive and we don't want our private thoughts shared with outside people. Everybody knows women love to talk and make her husband's sensitive issues community property. In other words, **men don't trust women with their feelings** because of tampering. Therefore men tend to shutdown, are reserved, and take their feelings to a psychologist or to the grave, whichever comes first. The biggest mistake men make is having his **single friends resolve his problematic marriage.** These bachelors have no clue, and therefore should not be called on for advice or even venting. Believe it or not men do cry. There's nothing wrong with bearded tears. **What is Bearded Tears?** It's a manly man in touch with his emotions and sensitive side. Every once in a while all men cry. I don't care how macho, cool, sexy, rugged or tough, they all still cry. Men should feel free to release those emotions in the comfort when being alone. **Never ever cry** in the presence of your wife, or she may label you as a punk. A man crying publicly can be defined as a sign of weakness. No woman wants her man to appear as a weakling. However, if you need to cry a river, do it alone. Some men try to suppress that emotion which turns into anger, aggression, and sometimes depression, which leads to heart attacks and strokes. I'm not suggesting that you call your buddies and have a Kleenex party, because that's crying publicly. Husbands should see crying as a way of cleansing the soul. What makes a man cry? A cheating wife, heavy debts, pressure and stress from work, loneliness, disrespect from peers and wife, and constant rejection of sex from spouse. I once heard my best friend say, "During the day I'm a manly man, but at night I cry myself to sleep." His emotions were based on a particular situation that he tried to change for the better in making this woman his wife. Unfortunately, he failed. However, he came out on top because he was in touch with his emotions. Attention ladies, in the event your husband sheds a tear or two in your presence just listen and not judge, then console and forget about the issue never to leave your lips. If you betray him and it becomes a press release, or you bring it up in an argument, you'll never get that man back mentally. He's gone for good when it comes to communicating. There's nothing you can say or do because you've lost his trust forever.

Its seven years later and you have learned that your wife can be your enemy as well as your best friend. She's the one person you'll find that **you hate and love** most at various times. Marriage is over-rated and usually ends before concluding the seven year itch. The **Seven-year itch** is like 100 miles of highway with no exits for refueling and you're running on empty. Many couples won't make it for the long haul because they lack creativity. Along the way there will be major blowouts, which the couple will have to fix flats with no assistance. The most natural reaction is to jump ship during a constant conflicting phase. Basically the couples are still jockeying for position and no one wants to submit due to selfishness. A wise woman of 75 years of marriage once said that each person has to contribute in the marriage and unfortunately someone won't contribute an equal share. That's what makes marriage unique. **A couple is counted as one unit, which breaks down to halves, and if one spouse lacks, they'll never be whole.** This effort alone makes many people hate marriage. Marriage is a life long project that is never completed. Couples whom have been married 20yrs and up have managed to give and take with disagreeable sacrifice. What are the symptoms of the 7-year itch? Loneliness inside the marriage, still lusting for the opposite sex in a hungry manner, constant bickering over ridiculous topics, still desire to hang out with single friends, couple don't respect each others livelihood or hobbies, and lastly besides sex and kids; they have nothing in common. Therefore you ask yourself, "Why did I marry this person? I should have married so and so!" In the seventh year couples are starting to play the roles without rebuttals and or opinions. However they still bump heads occasionally with quicker resolution. The biggest problem at this point is sex, because it's non-existent. Lack of sex can make a woman and or man fulfill needs outside their union. Usually by the time a couple reaches 10 years of bliss, they can read each other's minds rather bad or good. It's like studying for a test using the answer sheet. A spouse may get all the right answers even if they're in the wrong.

Trust is the most important factor in a marriage and it can be violated in many ways. The first betrayal of trust may come when a wife constantly denies her husband sexual gratification on a regular basis. When the couple married, the man trusted that his wife would submit to him sexually at all times unless she's on her period or fasting (**1 Corinthians 7:5**). Plain and simple, God said give it up! No argument there!

The worst violation of trust in a marriage is adultery. No man or woman should ever commit this damaging act. **Proverb 6:32, But whoso committeth adultery with a woman lacketh understanding: he that doeth destroyeth his own soul.** Usually in marriage, men are responsible for this cardinal sin. Men cheat for several reasons: Greed, boredom in marriage, kinky sex opposed to moderate with wife, attraction to physically fit women, mid life crisis, and selfishness. Truthfully, a man doesn't need a reason to wonder from his happy marriage, it may just be convenience. An argument can trigger an affair when the planets of adultery are aligned at the right time of a woman pitching an offer. The number one reason men cheat in marriage is because of mental weakness and lack of spiritual understanding. Wives can be just as guilty by today's standards and usually shocks her husband. A friend of the family informed me that his wife of twenty years had been cheating on him since day one with her ex boyfriend. Her sexual escapades were so conniving that anytime she wanted sex from her lover, she would pick an argument with her husband only to have him arrested. As soon as the police would depart with her husband she and her lover would have relations. This man of God was willing to forgive his wife and continue to build his family, as God would want. The last straw came when there was a discrepancy of his son not being his own. This man decided to have DNA testing done and luckily the child by his wife was his and not the lover. After years of turmoil with his wife, this God fearing man took ill to cancer, which probably stemmed from frustration and anxiety. The man learned of all the incidents that transpired from the now "live in lover" when calling to speak to his kids. The lover laid the history of key dates and times of incidents by filling in gaps of times and lost answers that he was once clueless. This devastated this God fearing man to the point where he wanted to murder the ex wife and lover. Would they deserve that? Maybe so, God only knows. The man picked up the pieces of his broken heart and asked God to mend his heart. I can tell you a dozen stories of people I know whom wives are openly having affairs. These men are usually working to hard to notice or just naïve.

RAIN ON

I HEARD A THUNDER LAST NIGHT
AND THOUGHT IT WAS A STORM
BUT I REALIZED IT WAS MY HEART GIVING ME A WARNING
THAT I WAS BEING CHEATED ON
I SAW LIGHTNING LAST NIGHT
BUT AT LEAST THAT'S WHAT I THOUGHT
BUT IT WAS THE PAINFUL SIGN OF MY WIFE
BEING CAUGHT
IT FLOODED LAST NIGHT RIGHT HERE IN THE HOUSE
I THOUGHT IT WAS FROM THE RAIN
BUT IT WAS OUR RELATIONSHIP WASHING OUT
I THOUGHT I HEARD A TREE FALL LAST NIGHT
RIGHT HERE ON TOP OF THE CAR
BUT IT WAS THE AGONY OF LIFE
KNOWING SOMEONE ELSE HAD SLEPT WITH MY WIFE
LAST NIGHT EVERYTHING WAS DESTROYED
THEN I LOOKED AT MY LIFE AND REALIZED
I STILL HAVE TWO BEAUTIFUL BOYS
RAIN ON

By Rhythm of Life

Another friend of mine suspected his wife of cheating but couldn't prove it. He decided to play detective. She broke his heart. They were high school sweet-hearts. He gave her the world. He bought her a $250,000 house in a rich Suburb and spoiled her rotten. Unfortunately, she didn't appreciate him. She did her dirt with a co-worker on frequent road trips in which her husband suspected foul play. Therefore, he started reviewing phone records, and credit card bills. There were frequent calls to the same numbers in which he called to find it was a male. He found proof of gifts she bought for her lover/ co-worker. During her next Rendezvous, the husband also planned to be out of town longer than she. The wife took it upon herself to cancel her staged trip and entertain her lover at home. The husband knew his wife all to well, and everything fell as planned. The husband returned home when he knew this house was vacant and awaited his wife and lover arrival. The husband sat in the garage with a loaded 9mm ready to blast them both to hell. When they arrived to the house in one car, the house was assumed empty. The barrel of a 9mm met them with a betrayed husband on the trigger. She pleaded and the lover denied his own existence. Once again, the husband being a God fearing man granted them mercy on their pitiful lives. They both were demanded off the property. The wife left empty handed. The husband filed for divorce and won, due to having proof of her infidelity. The judge gave her the house and all the bad debt accumulated with it. She was also ordered to take on all the couples negative debt she solely accumulated. She was also ordered to pay alimony and court fees. Adultery is all too familiar among the genders, rather male or female.

One day men will realize that God made the rules of marriage, the husband enforces them and the couple has to abide by them. Socially speaking, marriage is all about the wife, kids, the dog, and then the husband. These are the reasons why many men have problems with long-term commitments. It's too many strings attached and too many repercussions. I give kudos to those men whom have journeyed to the real world and manage to keep it together. Marriage is the hardest job a couple will ever endure in their lifetime in which the benefits are many if collaborated levels of success are achieved. My advice to any man contemplating marriage needs to prepare for a life altering experience that will **hopefully** change him for the better. There's something very cool about a man taking care of his family and living with a purpose. Nobody wants to be the "old guy" in the club; just to go home lonely and realize life has past you by. At least with marriage you get laid twice a month. Overall, Marriage is a good deal.

CHAPTER 6

Good House Keeping

$\mathbf{M}$ ILLENNIUM HUSBANDS ARE in for a rude awakening compared to what their fathers and grandfathers enforced in their households. Every since women burned their bras and fought for equal rights, good house keeping has declined damn near to the point of non-existence. **Some wives of today are lazy** and make excuses about not keeping a tidy house. The woman of yesteryear like my grandmother birthed 10 kids, in a 2-room shack in Mississippi. She knows all about good house keeping. She worked the cotton fields 12 hrs a day only to come home to cook, clean, and have sex with her husband. How do I know she had sex? She has 10 kids! That's an ideal woman. The women of today can't hold a match to my grandma. Now that women have ventured off into the workforce, the home life suffers a big void. Women should only be allowed two options in marriage. The first option is to be a fulltime mom that keeps a tidy home complete with ironing, cooking full course meals, grocery shopping, tending to the kids, be physically fit, providing sexual gratification with husband only, and keep tabs on bills due dates. The second option is working part-time or fulltime. If she works fulltime, the husbands should assist her on some duties but not take over her responsibilities. The wife is still expected to keep the house in order even if she works fulltime. **Women tend to get handicapped after marriage.** Before marriage women do everything for themselves from washing their car to changing their oil. Over a period of time their perfectly working hands turns into coffee mugs. One is for coffee and the other for money. Men whom grew up in a clean home can never find comfort in a pigsty. Therefore men, never adjust and never surrender to a dirty kingdom. More than likely it's probably her dad's fault for not teaching her the responsibilities of serving a man. The husband can teach valuable lessons to wives at this conflicting stage of marriage, sometimes. Many men have watched their mothers, grandmothers, and aunts juggle multiple children, jobs and household choirs to keep a happy home. The Women of today live in an era of Merry Maids, whom provide a tag team approach in keeping her house clean on demand. The best way to influence a wife in her duties is to lead by example. However, make it for a brief time in addition to your own duties. The downside of this experiment will cause her to brag to her family and friends on how well you do, with expectations for you to continue. These duties include cooking, cleaning, prepping the kids, grocery shopping, and finalize the day with hot passionate sex. Truth of the matter, men would do all these duties weekly if there was guaranteed sex at the days end. So what are the problem ladies? Women feel like they're the only one stressed in the world. When they get uptight, something or someone is not getting done! Usually that someone is hubby. If a man expects more attention from his wife, he has to pick up some of the chores on a regular basis. Whatever excuses she gives the hubby, he should eliminate the problem. Men and women daily agenda are so different but can be compromised effectively. Women want their lives to be hassle free of deadlines, completed itineraries, and a moment of serenity. Men want respect, cleanliness, order, passion, and sex on a daily basis. This is a long shot, but if the hubby minimizes her "to do list" by volunteering his services, there's a 50% chance of sex that night. Worst-case scenario, she'll sleep 100% better than the night before you started helping her. This experiment takes about 1 week-30 days to blossom. Consider it foreplay. Need I say more? Good house keeping is more than a clean home. Good Housekeeping is hot meals, hot sex, money, communication, and personal appearance.

Men must play their part in keeping good house as well and pitch in, but not take over. The list includes anything involving a wrench, landscaping, and automotive. If you're not a handy man, don't pretend to be. It will cost more to repair later. Some hubbies see themselves as a mechanic, to save money; she views him as wasting dollars. Also, the hubby should have a job, a business or some type of legal income. The title of Mr. Provider is no Joke! There's no romance without finance, and then it's a nuisance!

Health and physical appearance is the last phase of good house keeping. Women are the guiltiest of both. Women tend to think if they are not obese, they have no need to exercise. However, the cellulite disguised as cottage cheese on the back of the thighs tends to differ. So what you work fulltime, and tend to the kids! You still need to exercise. Some women are fortunate to still have their high school figure. Most women can't even see their own pink cotton candy anymore. Why? Sure, blame it on the kids for ruining your figure. That excuse is so sad when the kids reach kindergarten. Move your butts lady! Both of them! That includes the one in the front doubling as a stomach, and the original, which looks like a Plasma TV. Wide and flat! What happened? I'll tell you what happened; she quit! Some women have this tendency to get comfortable in marriage and let go of their sex appeal. When you were dating this beautiful size 6, she hardly ate. Now she's eating everything in site. The way she puts away a bon-bon makes you down right jealous. Then she has the nerves to ask, "Does this outfit make me look fat?" Be honest with her. "Sweet heart you need to shed a few pounds." After all, she's yours now, all 250lbs. If you can't be honest with her, no one can. Tell her what she needs to know and not what she wants to hear. Please be polite or you'll be missing that extra cushion on cold nights.

If women used half the effort in trying not to look fat compared to not being fat, there would be less adultery. Prime Example, a woman wants her gut to be smaller in time for her class reunion. She has 6 months to prepare. The logical thing to do is diet and exercise vigorously, right? Wrong! She'll spend the next 4 months searching for the right dress that will hide her bulges, saddlebags and gravity challenged buttocks to make her appear like a high school senior. The last 2 months prior to reunion is the most grueling; finding the perfect girdle to hide in, from her former self. Mathematically, with effort and dedication she could have lost 50 lbs easily before her deceptive night.

Weight loss and weight gain is all part of good house keeping. A good husband can be honest with his wife and hope she won't be in denial. Far too many times i've seen couples in public in which the husband wasn't honest with his wife. Any self-respecting husband will not allow his wife and mother of 5 to proudly display her trophy stretch marks openly with a tube top. The only two-piece she should be shopping for is at KFC. The woman has so many stretch marks on her stomach that she looks like a walking road map. Anybody need directions? Please don't misunderstand my opinions of a woman's body. Some things are just meant for the husband eyes. Why ruin other people's lunch? Men must realize that the wife is a representation of him, rather present or absence. Example 1. A wife goes to the store well groomed and casual with hair in place. She's classy and clean enough that when a mutual acquaintance sees her, there'll be a compliment in the report. Example 2. A wife goes to the store wearing yesterday clothes complimented with food stains while wearing a headscarf. This is not a good reflection on the husband or the marriage. This image gives the presumption that the wife cares nothing of her public image and self esteem. Plus it may lead people to believe your marriage is struggling financially and romantically. However, wives don't view their convenient attire that way. Believe it or not, men talk. We hate tacky representation. Long story short, men are attracted to things that are visual, sensual, erotic and classy. These are pretty much objects that influence men to marry. Under no circumstances should a woman start to appear homely. It's the man responsibility to ensure his wife hair and nails stay done. If need be, include her spa treatment as a monthly utility bill. After all, she's doing it for you! Unfortunately, everyone doesn't have the perfect body and we all eventually lose the battle of time when six-packs become kegs, and perky boobs look like grape fruits inside of socks dragging in the sand. Even then, the packaging should always look like Christmas morning. You just can't wait to rip it off! Husbands too, must work hard to stay sexy and appealing or be traded in for a newer model. Sure the newer models are smaller but they don't need much to go the distance.

CHAPTER 7

Romance and Sex

ROMANCE IS THE most important tool in a marriage. It's more than saying I love you occasionally. Romance is the cement foundation that loves stand upon. Romance is love without saying a word. It's the inexpensive corny things we do for one another that brings a smile from yesteryear. Romance is wearing your spouse's favorite colors or favorite outfit they like to see you display. Romance is that Saturday morning aroma of bacon frying after a night of hot passionate love. Romance is the sizzle that keeps the love burning deep within a union. It's that gaze into the eyes of your soul mate and realizing what they need before they ask. Romance is catering to your mates' ego at any given time without your obligation becoming a chore. The problem with romance is that it's a one-way street that should be a highway of love. Too many times the husband is left holding the bag when it comes to romance. Frankly **romance is only centered on women.** The husband is suppose to open all doors, pull her chair at dinner, remove and apply her coat, rub her feet after work, run her bath water, send her flowers occasionally, and plans all dates. That's all beautiful, but where's the romance toward men? Somebody forgot to tell the female gender that men need romance also. Men are simple when receiving reciprocity of romance. The most romantic gesture a wife can do is making her husband a plate at dinnertime, no matter the location or event. Men like to be catered to as well. We don't care about doors, and coats, and chairs being pulled for us. Secondly, we like to have clean underwear and socks available at all times. That's romantic! We as men also would like to have our bath water ran after a hard day work with a complimentary back scrubbing with minimal conversation. Silence at a peaceful moment is very romantic to a husband. Sometimes a man just wants peace and quiet with his wife nestled quietly under his arm. Romance is like being a waiter in a busy restaurant and the spouse is the only patron you're waiting upon. Romance means at your service. If the romance is satisfactory, there's a fat tip coming at the end of the night. No pun intended. Romance is the most humbling form of expression that a person can showcase in wooing their spouse into infinite ecstasy.

Most men don't realize that **romance is about 75%** of foreplay. The other 25% is just adding water and stir. Romance often leads to sex. Women are the gatekeepers of that point. A wife sees how far her hubby will go to entice her. That's perfect and in good fun. It adds zest. Men on the other hand are subject to waiting the sign of approval to go further. Romance and sex is two separate entities to women. It's one stop shopping for men. In romance, women are stating, "Show me you love me!" Some men only want to reap the rewards of romance without putting in the work. Shame on you men! If you prove your love to her, she'll show you 69 ways she loves you. Romance is the biggest neglect in a marriage, which often influences mates to wonder elsewhere. I challenge all men to stay creative in romancing your Queen. Women live for mystery, intrigue, passion and mind blowing orgasm. Men have a need to feel attractive and desired. Compliments play a big part in romance. Men need to know from their wives that they still have that swagger. Too many times **the other women** see this lack of your attention on his behalf and graciously satisfy that man sexually, financially, and emotionally. All while he's enjoying her deeds, he wishes it were his wife.

Wives have a tendency for needing romance but won't administer it in return. Romance is a large atmosphere that ventures into the bedroom. The bedroom is the make or break point for men. Husbands usually experience many let downs after a romantic evening here. **Example 1.** After a night of dinner, dancing, passionate kissing and soft whispers, the wife comes home and promises an IOU for the morning before she crashes to sleep. **Example 2.** The wife constantly sleeps in unattractive 2 piece pajamas that have no access for entry. In addition to the PJ's, there's a wooly mammoth housecoat tied tighter than Fort Knox. Also she tops off the PJ's with some ungodly head wear or rollers that make you think of grandma. That's not romantic. Ironically, she feels frisky. However, a wife that resembles a Bag Lady stunt double arouses no man. **Example 3.** The wife comes to bed wearing mixed signals dressed in a Camisole or thong, only to learn she has a headache or the kicker; "I'm only wearing this because I have no more clean underwear". These three examples are leading reasons why husbands don't buy into romanticism. Husband gets the shaft in the end. Husbands feel like all their hard work and pleasing will amount to nothing. This is why he rolls over and goes to sleep after sex; he's exhausted from the planning, waiting and waiting again. Take heed ladies!

Many husbands feel that they only get the shell of the woman whom actually exists inside. He mostly sees her in her moderate to decent stages. However, the world views her all dressed up, smelling good, sexy, and appealing. The husband sees his wife going into the world to show off his goodies. The sad part is what she showcases to the world, he barely can have. Therefore wives should make their husbands feel special and give him a private show. She should always appear sexy to him even if it requires some work. Men find it perfectly okay for wives to switch their look to what he likes or may not like. Even if he doesn't like it at first, it'll change after sex. He'll feel like he's having sex with a different woman. Her change in appearance can be as minimal as wearing make up, a wig, and new lipstick. This is what men find romantic as well. We don't ask for much.

Romance usually involves the woman throwing mixed signals at inappropriate times. Let's face it, cuddling means a prelude to sex especially if she wants to spoon. That's foreplay! Wives often accuse men of being too sex driven when they want to snuggle. Snuggling is sex with clothes. It's best to cut out the middleman. That's also an opportunity for the wife to show she can still be a tease. She still wants the thrill of the chase. Most times she wants to be close and nothing sexual. The other times she wants to test your manhood by being pursued and conquered. We as men have to play her game in flipping the romance switch to "on" and the sex switch "off." It's literally hard at times! But don't be overwhelmed by her interest in wanting to be caressed. The key is to play her little game and wait until she tells you what she wants, and then you won't be disappointed or horny.

Sex is the most abused topic in a marriage. It's rarely used beyond its purpose of making babies. There was a time before marriage when sex actually was used as a sporting event. As a bachelor you would pull a single (sex with one woman in 24hrs), or a double (sex with 2 different women within 24 hrs or twice in the same day with one woman). Then there's the Grand Slam when you have sex with 3 different women within 24 hrs and **then go home**. These particular stats are what men have to look back on now that they're in the Hall of Fame. Now, husband penis's just rests on the mantle in a glass case that says, "Break in case of Emergency." This former MVP, (Most Valuable Penis) sits idle, collecting dust next to Grandpa Jones ashes. The sad part, Grandpa gets his dust blown off more than you! Sex is not what it used to be. Sex for a husband is like a treat to a dog being obedient. It's like an occasional pat on the head. The only time sex is guaranteed; the husband's birthday, Fathers day, Wedding Anniversary and maybe July 4th. Jewish Hubbies may get more sex because they have more holidays, other than that, don't EVER count on it. In order to have sex with your wife, you have to be mathematics major. There are **52 weeks in a year**. The average woman has a period lasting one-week per month. All husbands' chances just **decreased 50%** for having sex with their wife on an average basis. There are **now 26 weeks** available for sex. Wait! Don't forget the one-week prior to her period, PMS. Husbands deduct another 25% from the sexual calendar. You're now **down to 13 weeks** availability for sex. Add in the interference from the newborn, toddlers or teenagers aka "The Blockers". You're **down to 8 weeks** of sexual time. Lastly, subtract all the times the wife has a headache, too tired, or not in the mood. You **have 4 weeks** that's allotted for you to show your skills. That's exactly one month of sex in a year. Word to the wise, spread your **sex voucher** through out the holidays and keep a few days for March and April. The wives don't usually count Easter even if you decide to get a rise the same day Jesus did. So sad but so true! Women wonder why all we think about is sex. We have 48 weeks a year to ponder our strategy that will probably last 2 minutes.

Sex can't wait. There are several sexual techniques that may ensure a husband to receive more sex. The first and foremost is putting the wife orgasm first. That's hard for many men to accept for reasons of stubbornness or premature ejaculation. Either way, there's a solution. All wives want to experience that intense internal gushing orgasm every time. The husband goal is to please her every which way imaginable. Many husbands are old fashioned by only pleasing themselves and leaving the wife to curl up with a romance novel and a dildo. Eventually this leads to a real life Fabio leaping off the pages of the book and into your sheets packing more than plastic. We as men need to explore the horizon and valleys of every mountain and cave she'll allow. When she finally permits it, be suave, sensational, and seductive. Like most men, husbands go directly to the clitoris. There is so much more to explore on this voyage to the treasure hunt. Think of it as digging for a buried treasure. The first stop is her eyes, by gazing. The second area is behind the ear with light strokes with the tip of the tongue in circular motion slowly sliding down to the neck. Usually, by the time you get to the shoulder all the tension is starting to leave her body. Now lightly bite the thin meat on her shoulder above her collarbone and suck in three-second intervals with a circular tongue in between. By this time her breast are beckoning to be caressed. Touch the breast but avoid the nipple since it has the most nerve endings. Now gently, kiss in baby breathes down to the outer nipple circle and ignore the actual nipple. Continue to breathe hot passion on to the outer nipples and lick in circular motions as you play musical breast going back and forth. There have been cases where women have experienced orgasms at this point and begin to beg for your entry. The next step, continue to make her wait, she made you wait! Immediately change the pace and race the tip of your tongue down to her-belly button and insert your tongue in and out. Don't mind the lint. Then slowly travel back up to her breast embracing one in each hand. Then engulf your wet lips onto each nipple and suck and lick and suck in a fast to slow then slow to fast motion. Be sure to make the succulent sounds, it creates ambiance and intensity toward her orgasm. Then slowly voyage from her breast with kisses down to her knees. Once you arrived at the knees, you have two options: the first is penetration; the second is licking her like a year supply of stamps. For those allergic to eating her seafood, lay in a T formation. She lies on her back with legs in the air, and the husband lies along her backside while penetrating her through the side entry. The reason for the position is to stimulate her clitoris in slow waves of ecstasy until she begins to peak upon orgasm. Then rub patiently and thrust deeply. This position is guaranteed the wife to experience an internal orgasm. The position is a method of patience and arm strength. For those who love a seafood buffet, go downstream. Upon returning north from her knees, start licking the inside of one inner thigh. Now that you have arrived at the inverted triangle, slowly kiss the clitoris, no tongue yet. Slowly apply the tip of your fingers to the outer lips of her essence. Rub in circular motions. You are preparing to give her the **One Hour Orgasm**. Starting at noon, begin communication with her clit by light licks of wetness, all while rubbing the outer lips. Your fingers will serve, as the hands of time, so don't rush it. Turn the tip of your finger slightly to the quarter after position inside her vulva. While you slowly rub the entryway of her inner wall, spell the alphabets with your tongue slowly on her clit. As you begin to **spell the alphabets** again turn the hands of time to the half past position. By now the moisture should be outrageous if you get past this part without an orgasm, don't worry. Gently insert the middle finger in a downward position all the way south in her vagina. Extend your finger southward and you should feel a bulb. That's her **K Spot**. Rub her K Spot in a circular motion doing the same with your tongue on her clit. She'll need the continuity. If she's moaning and panting heavy she may be ready to cum, you may need goggles. Now slowly insert two fingers at the quarter till position and stroke that inner left wall slowly up and down as you flick your tongue from left to right. Be sure to give her teased intervals of retracting your tongue lasting about 5 seconds each time. There's 15 minutes left on the orgasmic clock, now coast the two inserted fingers inside her vagina behind her clit. This area is called the **Clitoris Backdoor**. The Clitoris backdoor should be pressed periodically like a doorbell. Your fingers should press gently upward inside her vagina and landing on the backside of her clitoris. As you begin to suck her clitoris, gently press the backside of her clitoris into you mouth thus creating a vacuum leaving no air to escape her orgasmic chamber. The pressure should be firm but not hard. The suction from your lips should be isolated over the entire clitoris while the tip of the tongue speeds left to right traveling faster than the speed of light. Now briskly rub the backdoor of the clitoris faster and faster as your tongue compliments your movements. Take the free hand and place **two fingers above the pelvic** bone and press gently thus creating a damn. This makes her vaginal area so engulfed with sensations by filling her clitoris and vulva to double its size. The pressure of pressing internally and external on the clitoris usually cause the woman to physically **burst like a damn** with her spouting her female juices **upward and outward** in a great thrust. These orgasms are labeled gushers. If she comes like that, she'll need rest from the uncontrollable after shock. Orgasms that intense can scare a woman, because they loose all composure. That'll teach her to limit you to 4 weeks of sex a year out of 52 weeks. There are so many different tactics to make her reach her peak. Husbands have to learn what drives her crazy and do it well, then make her miss that thing you do! These particular moves should only be used on Mothers day, Her Birthday, Valentines Day, and Anniversaries. Never during football seasons due to possible neck and or eye injuries, can which hinder your game watching.

Wives take heed; believe us when we compliment you sexually. We like what you do when you do it and how you do it. Can you just do it more often? Wives view sex different than men. We as men view sex as a past time, like sports. We love sports.

Women see sex as a chore, like doing the laundry. They hate doing the laundry. Sometimes women don't hate sex. They just hate sex with their husbands. Many reasons come into play with women sexually retreating. Mostly women dodge sex because her husband is too selfish to satisfy her at all. Some husbands have bad hygiene, and she refuse to make love to a pig. Some women avoid sex because of health risk. Maybe her 400lbs husband likes to be atop his 100lbs wife and collapse after an orgasm only to leave her pinned gasping for her life. A man that heavy should strictly be rode like a hoarse. Some wives avoid sex because it's painful due to the thinning of vaginal walls, not enough foreplay, or the husband is well endowed. In the event of pain, the man must relax her totally and provide mental and physical lubrication. Mental lubrication is compliments and saying I love you. Physical lubrication is extended gentle foreplay and maybe KY-GEL. As far as the well endowment, I guess you have to get in where you fit in. But seriously, those of us with larger units should take it easy on them. They dream all their life of finding Mr. Big Stuff only to have him serve as a museum. She just looks at his penis in shock and awe and wish she could handle it all. Ladies be careful what you wish for! In addition to sex, oral sex may be totally out of the question especially if she has high blood pressure. Prime example, a wife has strict doctors orders to stay away from salty foods, balls included. Truthfully, more wives would provide oral sex if husbands would do better hygiene and stop serving there wives salty beef. All jokes aside, those couples that indulge in oral sex should equally contribute. Some wives appease their husbands orally just to say she went down. She may also pull the kids baby teeth but that don't qualify her as a dentist. In other words ladies be good at what you do rather you keep the change or spit it out. Women are drama queens when it comes to administering oral sex. It's not that serious. A short cut to make your husband arrive quickly is extra saliva, sexy talk, more strokes at the base of the penis, and most of all eye contact all while you churn like butter. More tongue and less teeth please! It's Plain and simple. Whoop there it is! All complete with no neck pain and or cramped hands. The time you spent complaining down below, you could be done and prepping dinner.

Sex should never be boring. However, as time goes on in a marriage it becomes planned, and less spontaneous. Husbands constantly want that fire and desire. Therefore, we must continue to find ways to implement the wives interest in our program and vice versa. If the wife constantly denies her husband, he may ponder upon a time of the Brides of Frankenstein when he was sexually fulfilled and not sexually frustrated. Those women of yesteryear will literally streak across his mind only to wish he was there again with Kinky Karoline, and Felitia Freakright. Why? He gets no attention from his wife strictly being a mom, or she's to career driven to take time for her husband. Sexually the husband becomes detached in which he ventures off into porn, masturbation or maybe even a mistress. Keep ignoring your husband and he'll go away. He'll possibly go to the arms of another woman. During his stages of sexual frustrations he'll fantasize every single woman he has ever had relations. This husband is emotionally cheating in his heart, but not with his bone. If the wife is lucky, he'll stop there. Some husbands get to a point of no return and become carefree indulging in an affair. Woman should take the time to listen to what her husband is telling her. The last thing a husband wants to receive from his wife is sexual rejection. The difference between a woman and a girl is simple. A real woman out to please her husband, will provide head to her husband while she's on her period to get him through the week. Those same great wives will give oral sex during the six-week waiting period after having a baby. A wife with girlish immature qualities will constantly tell you how selfish you are only to appease her own selfishness during those moments. If he's not mentally and spiritually strong, he may not wait for his wife to eventually come around. A patient husband can and will become impatient with a wife's constant sexual avoidance which may cause him to be fulfilled elsewhere.

Wives have no clue on how much power they posses when it comes to sex. The vagina has the ability to make a man come home early when she's on top of her game, and make hubby stay out late when she's slipping on her wifely duties. Her sexual power usually builds her riches, and also causes her to be poor in judgment. Men need to be honest with their wives and tell them the truth about feeling neglected. They should also question their wives about his conduct or progress report. Sometimes if a man does nothing, he'll get nothing in return. I think it's only fair that a husband tell his wife that he feels neglected and is starting to become attracted to other women. Ask her what does she plan to do about your new curiosity? More than likely, you won't get the verbal response that you seek. But you will start to see a positive change in behavior. Be sure to tell her that you're compensating fantasies of other women when you can't be with her. The truth hurts but it often brings about desired results. If she doesn't respond at all to your concerns, she may already be involved with another person. Therefore she doesn't care. No self-respecting wife wants her husband lusting for some other woman. Husbands be advised to make sure you have your game tight before you start demanding more sex. Bottom line, sex should be the pillars of the relationship and without strong pillars, the house of love will collapse. Sex should never be used as a negotiating tool in order to get progress from a mate. God, Good Sex and communication are the essentials of a long lasting marriage. Man and wife must decide what's best for your relationship. Husbands want plenty sex and wives want great sex. The barter here is quantity vs. quality. The best things for a husband to do is plan a romantic setting without phones, kids, and disturbances and just make love to her for a good while at her preferred pace. The most important issue of sex is to never let it get boring. If need be, take her outside of the bedroom and venture to the garage, the attic, the laundry room, outdoors, the car, and most of all, on the floor. She wants sex like a passionate 19 yr. old. Therefore take your vitamins men. In the event the proud husband suffers erectile dysfunction, seek; Viagra, Enzyte, Levitra, or the herbals Ali Tong Kat, Ginseng, or Yohimbe through your doctor. Sad to say, men need to put aside their pride on being impotent and make those sexual moments an eternal orgasmic adventure that will keep her wanting more. Women too need to put their pride aside and provide more foreplay to the man genitals. Although society tends to paint us as automatic, we sometime need motivation the same way we give it! If more wives returned the foreplay favor, the sale of sexual enhancement drugs would plummet. It's a shame that a man has to turn to a placebo or a blue pill to have the confidence to perform. When he does a good job and he makes you cum; give a standing ovation. After all, we constantly compliment the wives which usually lead us down a road less traveled. It seems once a man praises a woman for her performances, he set himself up for constant denial. Now she knows it's good to him, and he just exposed his weakness. When she does arrive on your level, ignore her advances as a tease, and then give her what she wants. Always remember, if husbands get sex when he wants it, it's just sex. But if the husband gets sex when she wants it, it's a surprise and extra special. Sometimes less is more and more is less. Be the man and make it fit for both of you in unselfish ways.

CHAPTER 8

Fatherhood

F ATHERS ARE THE **teachers of life** whom provide daily lessons of survival within changing conditions. He separates the good from the bad and reminds his children with discipline. He's the authority, police and priest of the household whom makes the rules. He's often viewed as the heel or bad guy to his immediate family. Good fathers are very much unappreciated in life and it usually takes decades to get the thanks and notoriety he deserves. There is no middle ground with a good father. Fathers come last in different scenarios of life, which usually leaves him unappreciated in the family structure.

Step Fathers

Step Fathers may have the toughest job of all fathers. Step fathers are to accept the wife and her children whom he did not father. The difficult part is once he accepts them as his new family; there are usually limitations for him disciplining her kids. Another conflict occurs when the absent biological father wants to intervene in the raising after being non-existence in the most impressionable years. Unfortunately, the biological fathers pride won't allow him to meet face to face with the step dad out of fear and self-doubt. The absentee father deals directly with the mother and weighs heavy on her with opinions that conflict with the husbands rules. The best thing the step dad can do is meet with the biological dad to eliminate the middleman, which is the wife. No man wants his wife manipulated from her ex-husband or ex-lover. This method will defuse all confusion from outside the home. The results usually follow in the step dad's favor.

It is the wifes responsibility to make sure the husband is **respected** in all aspects of this situation from the child and the ex. However, the step dad must stand firm on his word and rule his household without a mutiny from the step children assisted by the wife. **Bottom line, if they can't abide by the step dad rules, they should be evicted. That includes the wife!** It's all about **respect**, and this particular type of father is disrespected the most. Step fathers are mostly seen as a savoir with shelter, stability and finance. Therefore, his standards should never discount his way of life for wayward kids and for an undeserving wife. It's amazing how a "ready made" family can accept this new man and his material wealth but not his rules. If this "ready made" family had nothing before this step father stepped in because the real daddy stepped out, they should keep their mouths shut and enjoy the blessing. Step fathers should also give respect to the spouse and the kids in which he likes in return. He must treat those kids as if they were his own. And under no circumstances should a step father use the wife as a path to molest her kids. I can guarantee this man will feel physical wrath that may get him killed or jailed. If the step dad has teen or adult step children in which see he is physically abusing the wife, those kids will retaliate to protect their mother. That step dad is putting himself in a deadly situation regardless who started the altercation. Sometimes the kids are looking for an excuse to beat the step dad into a coma. Although these kids may follow his rules, they may despise him not because who he is, but who he is not. He is not their real father. Kids and teens are brutally honest by constantly reminding him that he's not their real dad, specifically during disciplinary action. Step dads are truly the man in the trenches and always the odd man out. Stay true to your self and eventually your stepfamily will stay true to you.

The Baby Daddy

"That's Just My Babies Daddy!" That title within itself is degrading. The label of Baby Daddy misrepresents true fatherhood. In most cases it means the father absolutely does nothing for the child. Usually these culprits are forced to take care of their kids by "Friend of The Court". This is utterly ridiculous that a man has to be threatened with jail time to provide for his kids. Undocumented pay arrangements turned sour and usually lead to court proceeding and garnishments of paychecks. Sometimes a mother's personal opinion of her baby daddy uses the court to ruin this man happiness by interrupting his finances. Not all Baby daddies are guilty of not providing. Some go above and beyond their call of duty without seeking a pat on the back. Still these disgruntled mothers seek money outside of the court by threatening to raise his payments if he doesn't provide additional "off the record" funds for her personal lifestyle. Men in this position should take the initiative and approach the Friend of the Court and set up his own payment before she does. The court tends to have more leniencies. The baby daddy should also increase his tax exemptions to at least 9 for Federal/State/City to offset the child care deductions. This strategic move will give you an increased weekly check instead of being frustrated at tax time. Unfortunately, tax season is a deadlock decision for the baby momma to file the kid(s) on her taxes. This can be a win/win situation for a disconnected family.

Men need to make a conscious decision of having protected sex or suffer the consequences of fathering a child whom will probably be a threat to society. We as men are so detrimental in the growth of our kids especially if we don't participate in their lives. When a mother refers to the man as the father in a positive manner, she usually implies that he is in that child life until the end. A baby daddy can also occur through an extra marital affair, which creates a "Love Child". A love child will suffer irreparable damages of self-esteem, trust and abandonment issues. The fathers of these kids are already married with children of his own family. This child will live most of their life in lies, shame, and unworthiness. The father has to sneak away from his current family to hold private birthday parties, graduations, recitals, and attend games. For whatever reasons the "Love Child" was spawned, they must be loved. I won't even attempt to tell a man what he needs to do concerning that child. Most men will keep this child anonymous to keep his current family together. Either one of two situations will occur; the husband will confess and raise the child openly as he receives resentment from his family and in-laws. This method will possibly result in divorce or separation. Secondly, confess to his wife and family of why, when and how this "Love Child" occurred in hopes of forgiveness over time. It's safe to say about 5% of married women will forgive her husband and someday except this child in his life, but not hers. No matter what the man decides, he needs to make sure that child is provided for and loved whole heartily. I have a special piece of advice to Baby Daddy's. When you do finally meet the right woman and you choose to marry be honest and upfront with her about all your kids and possible kids you may have in existence before you marry. Give her the opportunity before marriage to accept you and all your children. If she embraces you and your kids, then she's a keeper. Once you have informed her that you have kids, be sure she knows you provide for them. If she has a problem with that, dump her fast. She's only giving you a prelude to the future that she accepts you but not your kids. It's all or nothing! If your wife can't love your kids from your past, she will make you miserable down the road. She'll create a blockage between siblings and their half siblings, which can be damaging to fathers credibility. Her simple act of selfishness can be a matter of life and death of her own kids. An example would be if the married couple has adult kids together and one gets sick with a kidney disease and needs a transplant. The only person whom can be a kidney donor is the half sibling. The crossroad is, if the mother accepted the stepchild, and the half sibling and the sick sibling grew to love one another, the half sibling would probably donate their kidney. If the mother doesn't accept the stepchild, the children will never get to bond and grow together. More than likely, the sick sibling won't receive the kidney, which could result in death. **Any woman not willing to invite your child into your lives must be**

dismissed before marriage, not divorced! Men are so quick to include women as their wives even though she has 5 kids with 4 different daddies. When the shoe is on the other foot, either they run or just get your goodies until the next thing comes along. Then they go back and tell their friends that you're a good man but they don't foresee it going to far because you have outside kids. Men, demand your worth and stop discounting yourself!

The Expecting Father

When a first time father initially gets the word that he's going to be a daddy, his thought process about life races at 100 miles a minute. He'll ask himself if he's worthy enough to be a good father. Usually this is a cross road for many men. Most single men see it as a way out, and run from the responsibility. The real men stick around and make it work. Most men fear that they will fail at fatherhood as they did at other opportunities in life. The only way to fail at fatherhood is not being a part of their child's life in a positive way. Many expecting fathers suddenly realize it's not about them anymore. Sometimes a father "to be" receives an epiphany on what his life should become. As this man becomes a responsible man, reality starts to set in, as he gets closer to his child's due date. Some men have expressed the overwhelming fear of their untimely death. These expecting fathers will under go a complete lifestyle change from risky to moderate. Some men stop riding motorcycles, parachuting, mountain climbing, doing drugs, felonious activities, and sexual promiscuity. Men have reported they have dreamed of fatal car accidents and at the moment they were dying, their child was being born. Society only dwells on the fear and anxiety of an expecting mother, but never the nerves of the expecting father. These men want to witness the birth of the first child and be in the child's life.

During the first year of my marriage, I experienced these same emotions of fearing death. My line of work at that time only intensified those thoughts. At about the time my wife was 2 months pregnant; I faced death up close and personal. I was working as a bouncer in a rowdy Detroit night club. A gang of thugs took over the club and made it a point to beat down a patron on the dance floor into a bloody unconsciousness. Fortunately that night the bouncers out numbered the combatants. The bouncers begin to snatch these guys off the victim one by one and proceeded to fight with them in a long journey to the front door. The thugs picked the wrong club that night because the bouncers were dropping haymakers on these guys, me included. Just as the fight was beginning to fizzle out there was one last guy still stomping this victim on the dance floor. I stepped forward by yanking and tossing the bully from the victim. Just as I was helping the victim to his feet, I could see this same idiot bully from my peripheral vision rushing to blind side me. Immediately, I stepped back dropping the victim to the floor only to land a fierce right hook in this fools mouth. Bam!!!! This fool hit the ground so fast and realized he was punch drunk. I then grabbed him in a chokehold only to get to the front door and see my fellow bouncers still fighting. As

I'm shoving this punk out the door he turns to me with a mouth full of blood murmuring, "Big Fella! I'm killing you and all your boys!" I later found out by a co-bouncer, this guy was a leader of some notorious crew. Fifteen minutes later as the club was closing, this fool returns shooting through the crowd whom was exiting the building. The patrons started running inside the club again. Now as we have this gunslinger on site, we have a decision to make 1. Continue to hold the doors so he can't get in, and deal with the bum rush from the crowd, 2. Run and exit via the emergency doors and put the other patrons at risk. 3. Make a break to our vehicles and grab our guns, since the club didn't allow weapons inside. Before we could react, the police approached just as this guy neared the glass doors. Suddenly I saw my whole life flash before my eyes, a loud gunshot rang out in the crowd and the armed suspect fell dead right in front of me. The police shot him in the back. I immediately demanded my money and never bounced in a night club again. I proceeded nervously to exit by stepping over this ruthless killers body counting my money and giving thanks to God. Ironically, a week before my mother-in-law had a dream I was killed working in a night club. The split second thought of me not being able to see my unborn son was unbearable.

The best advice I can give to an expecting father is to be prepared for emotional ups and down over the next 9 mos. I know I was a nervous wreck when we were expecting our first child. I monitored everything my wife ate, wore and how she reacted to everyday life. Wives must realize that the expecting father is a bundle of nerves on edge. This hubby will pamper her like a queen. The expecting mother enjoys the royalty treatment. Many wives say they wish their husbands were like that all the time. Although that hubby might be at her beckon call, she will eventually rattle his cage. The times get more difficult for the hubby when she has craving for outlandish things. Most men see this as an act of nagging. She only wants it for the baby's sake. I learned this small annoyance turned favor in a matter of time. I managed to write down all my wife's craving, and then stocked up. The icing on the cake for me to develop a system is when she decided she wanted a fish sandwich from Alabama Fried Chicken on the deep eastside of **Detroit** at 1 a.m. on a Saturday. Needless to say, I headed out to the crime ridden location to be turned away due to them closing. I was so pissed because they weren't scheduled to close for another hour. Its funny how black folks can be late for everything but will leave early to be on time. I then headed out to their second location, only to find out they were only serving chicken. I convinced the cook to call in a fish sandwich to the west side location and I would be there shortly. It was an emergency; it's for my pregnant wife. Men please be sure to get what those pregnant wives want, never substitute! It's now 1:45 a.m. and I head to Alabama Fried Chicken on Detroit's West Side breaking the speed limit. Just as I was pulling up, they were locking the doors. Man, I begged and pleaded with them as I slid toward the ground hanging on to the door. "I'm the one that called in the emergency fish sandwich!" Please, my pregnant wife needs this sandwich and I can't go home without it! They had no sympathy and obviously had no compassion for my situation. They said, "You took to long!" I said "I took to long!? That was record time!" I somberly walked back to my car and pondered a fish plan. "Where can I get a fish sandwich at 2:15 am and not get killed in the process?" Young's barbecue! I jumped back in the car, racing back to the deep eastside to Young's and I'm desperate for fish, fish nuggets, fish eggs, hell anything fishy. I arrived right before they were locking the doors and there was a very hefty woman in front of me. I was then called to place my order, only to find out this hungry lady ORDERED THE LAST FISH SANDWHICH! DAMN! Immediately, I offered this woman $20 for her fish sandwich, and she looked at me like I was a freak. She said "Sir, I'm out here late at night getting a fish sandwich, did it occur to you that I have a taste for this?" I said, "My wife does too! She's pregnant, please! I'll pay you!" Big Bertha gave me a firm "NO!" I started to bum rush her but I was too weak and tired to take the sandwich and run. The clerk tried to sell me some old rib tips. I asked the clerk, where can I get a fish sandwich this late? He said, "Go to Greens Barbecue on Mack and Bewick". I said, "Damn, that's in the hood". He said, "So is your fish Sandwich!" I reluctantly headed to the deep deep eastside, the land of no return. I was either very supportive of my wife cravings or just insane and wanted peace in my house. As I'm cruising down Mack Ave, I'm witnessing so much illegal activity that I was becoming paranoid. I saw prostitutes tricking, crack heads puffing pipes, a small scuffle between some vagrants and not one cop in sight. I then pull into this very dark parking lot that is perfect for a potential car jacking. All of this for a damn fish sandwich! However, the aroma of barbecue, fried chicken, and fish reminded me of my mission. I entered the building, waited my turned and ordered with no delay. It was perfect, until I attempted exit the building. There was gun fire nearby! POP! POP! POP! BOOM! First thought through my mind is "I'm going to die with a fish sandwich in my hand. I can't believe this S#*T!!" I waited several minutes as the owners were trying to rush people out for closing. Then there was a moment of silence. I ran as fast as could very low to the ground imitating a giant midget. The shooting started back rapidly. I then nestled the fish sandwich under my right arm as I performed a one arm bear crawl to my car door. I nervously fiddled with the keys. I crawled into the car started it up and drove like a mad man hoping not to get hit by a stray bullet. All jokes aside, I was trying to survive for my unborn child. Two and half hours later at 3:30a.m., I arrived home feeling proud of my accomplishment. I couldn't wait to watch her eat this fish sandwich, knowing the sacrifices that it took to get it home. I proudly strutted in the house with dirt and grime from the expedition only to discover she was sleep. I then awoke her thinking, "She's going to eat this sandwich!" She roles over and says, "Thanks baby, but you took to long I don't want it now." I quietly, but angrily turned and walked to the kitchen and put it in the refrigerator. I learned a valuable lesson that night when you're an expecting father. Early the next day I went to Alabama fried Chicken and bought a dozen fish sandwiches and froze them. I also went out and bought all her favorite cookies, snacks, juices and chips and left them in the trunk of my car. I was prepared for her cravings the next time they hit. When she would ask for me to go and buy her some goodies, I would already have them. However, I would pretend that I was all over the neighborhood searching for her goodies, just so I could get some quiet time. Inadvertently, she got what she wanted and I got what I needed; Tranquility. I advise all expecting fathers to be sure to cater to them and give them what they want, but get what you need in return. It will do you both justice in the long run.

As the months drag by in this eternal pregnancy, many husbands start to feel abandoned. I strongly recommend the first time "fathers to be" to accept all the sex he can when she's giving it up. Many hubbies feel that it may hurt the baby. In fact sex is actually good for her vaginal walls and in later stages can induce her labor. I can recall all the lemans classes with breathing and stretching. It was very sexual in a weird way. There comes a time when these hubbies fear sex could damage the baby. This new rejection toward the mother sparks her feelings of being undesirable and or fat. Show her the attention she requires and bang her vulva like a drum, the worst thing that can happen is the child will have irresistible dimples. There are no cases on file that a baby was born with dents in their head from sexual pounding. However, some kids are born with lopsided heads, which may come from the same sexual position during pregnancy. Pregnant sex is like cooking a steak; they both need to be flipped to ensure they are well DONE.

After several months of pain, discomfort, and anguish, he is mentally and emotionally tired from her being pregnant. When the due date gets down to the wire, all the husband can do is prepare for the worst case scenario and pray for the best. The first step is to ensure both of you have a fresh change of clothes, and hygiene products in one suitcase. Secondly, always make sure the car is filled with gas or no less than half a tank. Third, make sure all vehicles are in working order in case of emergency, with a planned route. Finally, make sure the wife has all numbers she can contact you in case of labor. This includes keeping cell phones, and or blackberry systems fully charged. Unfortunately for some hubbies, wives now have GPS on cell phones and or cars. In other words, you'd better be where you're supposed to be! Right by her side! Once the labor pains hit, so does pandemonium. When my wife went into labor with our first son, I thought I was prepared. I didn't factor in Murphy's Law. When her water broke, it was so minimal that it didn't appear she was in labor. She had no pains with almost invisible water breakage. It was so hot that day; we didn't have a/c in our home. She thought she was sweating in the seat of her pants while sitting on the leather chair. Again, we were expecting a puddle and major pains. Later that evening she started to get pains, not realizing she was in labor from the previous moisture aka "Water broke". We called the doctor and they advised me to time the pains and once they became 5 minutes apart, bring her to the hospital. I called my mother-in-law and she came immediately from her home on the next block and we loaded the car. I'm sitting solo in the front and my wife and her mom were in the back. I began to start the car, and the car was dead! I tried it again, and it killed the battery. I started panicking. "The car won't start! We won't make it in time! What are going to do?" My wife calmly replied, "Let's take my car." I reluctantly said, "I was just going to say that." Man, I was so embarrassed because I lost my cool (-100 cool pts), and she was so relaxed. Damn, I'm supposed to be the cool one! Any way, we switched cars and she started right up. I briskly drove the residential streets to get to the freeway just as the red train lights started flashing. "Damn, I can't believe this s*#t!" There was only one way to the freeway and it was over the tracks. I wanted to run the barricade just as they were lowering, but didn't want to risk our lives or me delivering the baby. This train took the longest 5 minutes to complete. Once it passed, I put my hazard lights on and drove every bit of 85mph to get to the hospital which was about 12 miles away. My mother-in-law was comforting my wife and telling me, "Slow down before you kill us all"! She was right, but I was driving. Thank God we made it there safely. Immediately, they admitted here and told us that the small moisture she seen earlier that day was her water broken and not perspiration. It was hard to tell since it wasn't a gushing puddle. Soon after our arrival, the labor became more intense. My wife became more evil and just belligerent toward me. I became so offended that selfishly I was satisfied every time a labor pain hit. It was usually best when she was snapping at me in mid sentence, and then boom! Screeching pain! Although those moments short lived, her agony was justified for cruelness over the past 9 months up until delivery. I recently informed my wife that I actually got some joy from her pain due to the mean attitude she gave me. She was a trooper I must admit. She really wanted to do the delivery natural with no drugs. Six hours into labor, the pain became unbearable. I requested the doctors give her an epidural to numb her below the waist. After 17 hours of painful labor, she delivered our first son.

Delivering a child is the closest experience to death a woman will achieve. At that precious moment of her pushing the baby into this brave new world is the scariest moment of a new father. The first two things that goes through his mind is he hopes his wife makes it, and the second is that the baby is born alive. There's a moment of uncomfortable silence in which Murphy Law is prevalent. Until that doctor announces you have a healthy baby boy or girl, you feel as if you're stuck in the matrix. The expecting father will visually watch the expression on each doctor or midwifes face for any revealing information. He'll also watch his wife for consciousness as well as increased activity on the infant/mom heart monitor. This especially holds true if the father is helping in the delivery. The expecting father is now on edge because he's worried about his child and wife. I remember that moment all to well. Just as my wife was pushing, there was a problem. I had seen it in the doctors' face. The infant heart rate had increased, and the mid-wife became frantic. Suddenly, the mid-wife announced the baby was choking. I took a deep breath and prayed. The more my wife pushed the baby out the tighter the umbilical chord became on his neck. The doctors' immediately discussed breaking his collar bone to get him out alive. They were also concerned he would rip her private area in its entirety. Immediately, the mid-wife suggested a maneuver that would save my wife and child pain. Once his head was out, they pulled the umbilical chord upward and the baby outward into the world. Just as a sigh of anguish, the doctors' cleaned our baby off, briefly let my wife hold him, called a code blue to rush him to Henry Ford hospital. The doctors' approached me with these words,

"There's a good chance your son will die from cardiac arrest, and his heart rate is 200 bpm due to an infection on his lungs from the embryonic sac." My wife's water never completely broke, and the remaining fluid caused my sons illness. When this doctor approached me with this depressing news, I immediately started crying just like I am now as if it were the first time I heard this. I made my first fatherly decision by signing off on the hospital papers for the doctors to do everything they can to save my child. My wife was barely conscious when she briefly held our son, before they rushed him away. I don't wish that experience on any new father; it was rough and difficult to talk about to this day. That was almost ten years ago. Once we arrived at the hospital, the nurse gave us an untraditional photo of our son hooked up to a breathing machine, in the event he died. I had my mom, dad, mother-in-law, father-in-law, step father-in-law stayed with our son in 24hr shifts. My family and in-laws created a bond that day of solidarity that this child will live. We prayed for my son around the clock for a week straight. Each day his heart rate decreased to normalcy. Finally, the doctor announced he is out of the woods and will live a healthy life. All praise to God! I knew from that moment that fatherhood was going to be a job of dependency and responsibility. I accepted the challenge.

The Family Man

The family man is a combination of a supportive husband and nurturing father. He is everything his family expects and nothing he ever imagined. Reality of family life sets in once the first child is brought home. The husband, once center of attention is now becoming null and void. All the attention surrounds the wife and the newborn. The man will begin to feel invisible and or unwanted. Most men have reported feelings of neglect even some animosity for the baby. How can a husband be jealous of his newborn child? It's simple! The wife no longer has time to caress the husband chest because she burping the baby. This new mother is now changing diapers when she used to pull off the husbands pants for a"nooner". The new father only receives the chemically imbalanced version of the woman whom used to adore him. She now has no time for hubby in her schedule. Don't even mention sex! It's not happening! A new father will find himself becoming insanely jealous when his wife is breast feeding the infant on the new and improved, **upgraded "fun bags"**, which should say adults only. As the husbands sits and admire his wife nourishing his young child, all he can think about is her increased breast size. At that very moment, wifey looks like a gorgeous porn star wasting her time with someone whom doesn't have a clue what to do with those "Tig Ole Bitties". Sure the new guy gets to gnaw, suck and chew her nipples, and your job is standing guard. A wise husband should immediately do role reversal and pitch in. The more hubby does the less she'll complain. This work will include cooking, cleaning, grocery shopping, tending the baby in the wee hours, and being supportive of her Post Pardon Syndrome. I recall my first son and his erratic sleeping. His sleeping kept my wife and me at war because the one had more sleep than the other. I remember one night the baby awoke and I nudged her to tell her the baby is crying and she said, "Man I know! I carried him for 9 months, you get him! You got some catching up to do!" Men, she had a valid point about the 9 months. Hell her job was easy; I have to carry him for 18 to 25 yrs. Men keep in mind you must check your emotions and starve your sexual hunger at her time early motherhood. Men too experience an emotional and chemical imbalance; it's called PDS (Penis Deprived Syndrome). PDS can occur during the wife pregnancy at a time when she doesn't feel desirable. If PDS occurs, the husband can be seriously frustrated. The Penis Deprived Syndrome can last anywhere from 6 Months of pregnancy, until menopause. However, in the later stages of PDS a man can be cured if his wife doesn't kill him during menopause. After all the hot flashes, emotional outburst, evil eyes, and an empty nest syndrome, she is ready to jump his bones. Too late! Osteoporosis beat her to it!

All men should have the opportunity to experience being the family man and see how his better half lives. Raising a child will take a team effort. Remember there is no I in team, but there is one Penis. Seriously, all male egos must be put aside for the growth of family. A new father ego will remain the same, but it will be guided with morals and values. It takes a while for a Bachelor metamorphosis into a Real Man. Real Men change diapers with pride, push strollers with honor, and tote flowered diaper bags in public. You don't loose cool points, because the game is over. You have won the lottery of life. You are in the Family Man Zone!

Raising Kids

The easiest way to raise kids is to remind yourself, that you were a kid. My father reminds me of that fact every time I call on him for fatherly advice. The first thing out his mouth is, "well son, you weren't always this macho." Then he makes me relive some event I totally forgot about and then gives me a suggestion on how I should rear my sons in that particular situation. Discipline is the key to raising kids. The backlash of discipline is always left to the father. The kids grow to know him as the punisher, the grumpy old man, and the executioner. Fathers must take a strong stand by laying the foundation for discipline. Sentencing should never be over-ruled by the wife unless the husband is completely physically or verbally out of line. A stern father will find himself as a lone man on a deserted island. The same support system it takes to raise a child will also be against you and your decisions. The fathers' word should be strong and unmoving. There will be times when your in-laws and wife don't agree with your form of punishment. Punishment and or spankings are very necessary to save that childs life.

Proverbs 23:13-14 "Withhold not correction from the child: for if thou beatest him with the rod, he shall not die. Thou shalt Beat him with a rod, and deliver his soul from hell." Well, I know my brothers and I are going to heaven, because we got some serious beatings. Those beating made us better than our peers, and successful men. Wow, God said beat them bad kids! He didn't say put them on timeout, stand in the corner, nor did God say let the courts dictate how you raise your kids. The court system needs to stay out of those households whom are doing the right things. That's the problem with kids today, they have to much leverage. Fathers must maintain a biblical and old school way of raising a child. **Some** offenses a child commits only require just communication. Never make threats, but promise consistent discipline. Usually the father will provide consistency in discipline whereas the mother lets them go wayward. The mother never wants to see her child in pain. The child's pain is her pain. When a father punishes a child there will be times of a cold front. Never take the wife's despising personal. It's best to let her resolve her own problem with the consequences. Corrections are a big business. Corrections start with the father. If the father fails at correcting his child, the prison system will step in his place. A good father needs to be assertive, consistent, dependable, gracious, stern and merciful.

Raising Boys

Fathers must teach their boys to express their emotions and always react in an appropriate fashion. It's imperative that boys are taught to respect women, and to never respect anyone whom doesn't respect them in return. Boys should be groomed to be perfect gentlemen in chivalry. A son is a representation of his father. A Good son makes a proud father. A son should be taught that women are treated as the gracious gift of life and not a sexual breeding ground. In addition, all women aren't ladies.

Raising boys is a constant test. You have to always be on alert for sissy traits. No man has any business raising a punk. The best thing a father can do to shake the wuss from his son is put him in sports. Fathers be sure it's a sport he likes. Fathers must be sure not to relive his failed athletic days through his son. It's okay to push your kids in sports but don't shove. If fathers try to shove a sport on him he hates, he'll grow to resent the father. No father wants to be resented. I remember my middle son constantly begging me to sign him up for wrestling. I found a wrestling team and we attended for two weeks, and he told me he didn't like it. I asked him why and he said it was boring. We were in the car driving onward to wrestling practice and I asked him if he wanted to quit. He said, "Daddy I don't like wrestling, but I'll do it if you want me to". I told him that he has to make that decision. He decided no and then requested we make a U-turn to Mc Donald's. I supported him and understood. I explained to him that he is not a quitter. Sometimes in life we experience things we don't like and want a change. Kids should have that same choice. Boys today are far more mature than our generation due to the media. Boys are very sneaky. It's best to limit your boys to certain time for TV, X-box and radio. They'll learn to appreciate it as a privilege. The media is soaking our kids with mature images at peak hours of teen and adolescence viewer ship. It's the father's responsibility to monitor and shut down any potential inappropriate material. One thing leads to another. They watch the rump shakers on TV and next thing you know they're curious about sexuality. Fathers have to cut the crap, and tell their boys the truth about sex starting with wet dreams through sexually transmitted disease.

The best advice a father can give is tell his son to abstain from sex until marriage.
Although, a father must be realistic with his son and tell him if he can't abstain, then
practice safe sex. My past experience has taught me that sex is overrated and often
abused. No man wants to be a grand father before 40 yrs old. The three biggest
challenges of raising boys is keeping them out of jail, forbidding teen fatherhood, and
raising a disrespectful son. A father must instill fear in his son heart from the day he is
born to respect his father, always! I've always had the utmost respect for my father,
but one day I decide to challenge him. I was 15 yrs. old standing about 6'4" and 160
lbs. Dad had bought us some 8 ounce boxing gloves for Christmas. I had beaten all the
light weight kids in the neighborhood and was seeking a heavy weight. I approached
my dad upstairs in our family room while he was talking on the cordless phone. I had
my gloves on dancing around while my mom and brothers were watching TV. I gave
dad a pair of gloves and said, "Put these on old man, I think I can take you!" My dad
was still on the phone, he proceeded to put only one glove on. He's still talking on the
phone I'm ducking from left to right and all of a sudden he hits me dead center of my
chest. BOOOM!!!! Dad knocked the hell out of me. I flew back 10 ft. I tripped over the
phone line, and then fell into the arm of the couch, which I broke. Finally, I flipped
over the broken arm of the couch to be greeted by our steep stair case. I tumbled
down the stairs in sheer embarrassment. I thought I would finally stop falling but the
momentum threw me out the back screen door where I finally landed on the porch.
My momma and younger brothers were laughing so hard that they were crying. I
was crying too, not from laughter. Daddy peered from atop the stairs and said, "Son
if you ever whoop my a$$ I'll leave, but don't ever come outside". I knew right then
never ever challenge daddy. Set them boys straight in the beginning and they'll always
respect you. Unfortunately, at the time you're teaching him he'll think you're an idiot.
But when he is grown, he'll realize and acknowledge you as the world smartest man.
That's my daddy.

Raising Girls

Raising girls properly is detrimental to society future. It's very important that a
father gets all the influence in he can before she turns the age of twelve. Girls are
Karma in disguise. For all the girls daddy did wrong in his past, he should school her
on how to protect herself from the dogs of life. Her little hugs and kisses will soon
turn into rebelling and despising. Fathers must prepare for the moment when she
loved your words of encouragement. Now she's older and chooses to listen to some
boy she met yesterday. This boy will have more influence over her than you. Prepare
yourself. Teach her to respect herself and be real. Teach her to make men treat her like
a lady and she in return treats him with respect. Treating him with respect is something
that is earned. Teach her not to be a sucker for sex or trinkets, nor be a judgmental
brat toward the guys she not attracted. Teach her to stand for something and not fall
for anything. Teach her to be independent, but not arrogant. Teach her to do twice the

listening and half the talking. Teach her to accept constructive criticism from her superiors without being offended. Teach her that money is not more important than, love, life and being alone. Father, your time is limited. Therefore teach her all you can, while you can and her future husband will be a happy man.

CHAPTER 9

Will the Real Men Stand Up!

I T TAKES MUCH sacrifice for a man to give up his exciting bachelor life. Men do have a problem with commitment to just one woman for the rest of his life. Most men will agree the process is very un-natural. We as humans are just like animals when it comes to mating and rearing our young. Unlike the Deer, we're supposed to be monogamous according to the bible. Even when a man is searching for a wife, he's not sure if he wants to settle down. Most want to start a family out of boredom of their humdrum life of sleeping with several different women, and no responsibilities beyond themselves. It's purely insane. Why get married? That's the million dollar question that has no right or wrong answer. Before any man decides he want to marry, he should begin to pray daily for a wife. Why prayer? If man goes out looking for himself, it will be disastrous. It's like buying a car. If you buy a used car, you're gaining someone else headache. Praying to God for deliverance of a wife is like a vehicle coming straight off the assembly line, with no recalls. She'll be designed to fit your make. I know plenty of guys whom went wife shopping without consulting God; needless to say they ended up with a Lemon. Unfortunately the Lemon law doesn't apply to useless wives. If you return her, exchange or trade up it will cost you half or everything you own. Marriage is the biggest investment a man will make in his life time. Marriage is a business with minimal and sometime no returns. Married couples will tell a dating couple all types of falsehood of how "good marriage is"; "It Ain't All Good!" Marriage is over-rated when it comes to the big house, dog and picket fence. It takes years for some couples to elevate their marriage. However, the quickest way to jump start a marriage solely relies on the man. Men make sure your credit is good! Try your best to maintain a good job or stable career. It would be very wise to have $5,000 in your personal account never to be revealed. Bring an additional $5,000 dollars to the joint account on the day of marriage. This $5,000 is just security funds to make her feel at ease. Already, you're ahead of the game. Next, be the Knight in Shining Armor and provide the Queen with a Castle. This Castle must be purchased before the vows or you're walking into a problem marriage. The several **"PREPARED"** steps mentioned have just eliminated 7 years of arguing and bad marital advice. The position of the husband requires the man to see potential problems ahead of time, solve them quickly, keep them anonymous, and never speak on them as long as you live. A wise man once told me, "so go, you go, and the marriage shall go'. Always be the man."

A wise bachelor should read female magazines for insight on the female psyche. Contrary to popular belief men don't have a clue on what women have in mind. It's perfectly normal to get in touch with your feminine side. It won't make us female mind readers, but we will be in the loop. Men need to investigate and interview possible wife candidates. If need be, hire a private investigator to do a background check. You'll be surprise of the secrets women walk around with. It would be a terrible tragedy to find out your wife was once a guy. "That's why she can't have kids!" Duhhh?? You should also request baby pictures, see medical records, talk to old friends, high school chums, and recent friends. Be brave and find out who her enemies are, then talk to them. The enemies will give you lies, but all lies have some portion of a hidden truth. In the event you find something alarming, confront her ASAP. Be sure to get a full explanation with proof of the truth. Once you get past the preliminaries the next step is premarital counseling. Premarital counseling is designed to discourage the wrong couples to marry. Marital counseling should preferably be with a pastor, minister, preacher, and or rabbi. These spiritual leaders will define the roles in marriage according to God will. If you're a non-believer, you're still part of God's Omnipotent plan when you marry. Marriage is a spiritual bond rather you like it or not.

The Divine Order is Man, Woman, and child (**1 Corinthians Ch. 11:3**). Too many times it appears as woman, child, and man. Divine Order is the pecking order in which a marriage should be organized. In order for this arrangement to be effective, man must be one with God. If not, the marriage is a disaster from hell in the making. Keep God first in the marriage and she'll have no choice but to respect her husband. If man honors God, he will honor his wife. Divine Order accounts that both parties appear as one.

Always run the marriage as a business and the money matters will properly fall into place. Never let the woman lead but don't be afraid to listen to her ideas. The man is the head of the house hold, and she is the neck. Without a neck, it's hard to see what's going on around you.

The best solutions to resolving an argument is taking the high road and ask yourself, "Do I want to be right or Do I want to be happy?" More than usual, if you have a need to be right, the argument will ensue. Always make your point followed with factual information based on evidence. If the argument is at a yelling point, gently grab her hand and pray. Don't make your prayers sarcastic but sincere. Pray for that moment of conflict and resolution. Another way to temporarily resolve an argument is being tactful by using the passion in the air for making mad passionate love to your wife. However, be sure to pray afterwards and the pursue pillow talk with conflict management. You can avoid her traps for potential blowups because you know her clues.

Husbands do all you can to resist temptation of adultery whether in the physical or mental realm. If you have already done so, then ask for forgiveness, and then forgive yourself. God will forgive you but you can't continue to do dirty works and beat yourself up over them. Repent! Pick up the pieces, and move toward the scripture. A loose woman is a pathway to hell. She might be everything your wife is not, but she is not your wife. This loose woman may be more than you expect, the **enemy** himself. Beware!!! Those situations always end disastrous. Stand tall and tell your wife what you need, expect and want. Tell her Thee Uncomfortable Truth! However, you must be realistic.

When a man stands up for his family, divorce is not an option. Adultery is the only time divorce is allowable. Build the trust and make it work for the kids, after all it's not about you anymore. Being a real man will place you in harms way of mental anguish and criticism for staying in the trenches. The kids are safe in trenches with a real man. The kids are the glue that holds marriage together.

In conclusion, being a real man is standing like a pillar without being moved. More men need to stand up for the challenge. A real man posture reaches the heavens and a slothful man existence disappears in Quick sand. Which one are YOU?

EPILOGUE

I HOPE WOMANIZER was an enlightening learning experience. My intentions were to teach, humor, and tantalize your soul with what the average bachelor and husband is thinking. I hope that you grasped my random thoughts and embrace them to use them within your life. I know that if God changed this former WOMANIZER, he can change anyone. Believe me, I was the worst of the worst. Therefore, there is hope for all mankind. We men just need a little encouragement and patience from our female counterparts. Lord Bless us men, we need all the help we can get.

P.S. After I completed this book at midnight April 29, 2005 I went to sleep for 2 hrs and 45 minutes. I experienced the most awesome vision of God's Grace on my past WOMANIZING experiences. I was literally taken on a tour of my life through a dream showing me my former lust for money, fame and women. In the conclusion of the dream I returned to an apartment where I'm cheerful and on top of the world. Immediately this fear of retribution came upon me and I began to run. I noticed a female figure lurking in the shadows; I then turned to run the other way. I thought I lost this woman as I walked into a bright room. It appeared to be a clean hospital lab room. I'm confidently leaning against this wall, when this woman with no face approaches me and says, "Bang-Bang, Stab-Stab, you're dead. I then chuckled and said "Whatever lady". All of a sudden there are two men in the lab. One man is talking to me in medical terms and then says "there's another guy here just like you! Yeah, he's dead and so are you." The second man is grossly disfigured and he's pushing a gurney. I began to run again, as the first man puts on his doctor coat and gloves. The man with the gurney catches me from behind in a manner that the gurney hits me, and I land atop. Immediately, my body starts to decompose. This doctor is prepping me for an autopsy and I'm paralyzed. The doctor has now grabbed an electric saw and began to crack open my sternum as blood goes everywhere. Just as I'm fading to black, this woman with no face appears and she began to take on images of women in my past womanizing days. Although I'm dreaming, I can feel my heart rate decrease drastically from where it was ready to burst in my chest. I lie in my bed listening to my heartbeat beating slower, and slower, and slower until it's just about to stop and then I heard **a commanding voice** say, "Get Up! And Go tell this!" I was terrified. I awoke and opened my eyes. I rushed downstairs to add this vision of what I was shown. I had already printed what I thought to be the final copy. When I grabbed the paper from the printer, this portion of the book was printed in RED. Although, the cartridge ran out of ink, it ironically symbolized GOD getting his point across as we see it in the Bible (red writing). That dream was God's Grace and Mercy of my wretched ways and he shown me what was supposed to happen. God forgave me and the red writing represents Jesus blood. I have no clue of which men God is trying to reach. I just realized that I was a vessel he worked through. I had no intentions of preaching to folks but wanted to enlighten others about men frustrations. This book is what it is, and it's the truth. Can you handle the truth?

Printed in the United States
123222LV00005B/85-210/P

9 780970 388155